CHINESE-ENGLISH
ENGLISH-CHINESE
(MANDARIN)

DICTIONARY &
PHRASEBOOK

D1089648

Hippocrene Dictionary and Phrasebooks

Albanian
Arabic (Modern Standard)
Armenian (Eastern)
Armenian (Western)
Australian
Azerbaijani
Basque
Bosnian
Breton
British
Cajun French
Chechen
Chilenismos
Croatian
Czech
Danish
Dari *Romanized*
Estonian
Farsi *Romanized*
Finnish
French
Georgian
German
Gujarati *Romanized*
Hawaiian
Hebrew *Romanized*
Hindi
Hungarian
Ilocano
Indonesian
Irish
Italian
Japanese *Romanized*
Korean

Lao *Romanized*
Latvian
Lithuanian
Malagasy
Maltese
Marathi *Romanized*
Mongolian
Norwegian
Pashto *Romanized*
Pilipino (Tagalog)
Portuguese (Brazilian)
Québécois
Romanian
Russian
Serbian
Sicilian
Slovak
Slovene
Somali
Spanish (Latin American)
Swahili
Swedish
Tajik
Tamil *Romanized*
Thai *Romanized*
Turkish
Ukrainian
Urdu *Romanized*
Uzbek
Vietnamese
Welsh
Wolof (Gambian)

CHINESE-ENGLISH
ENGLISH-CHINESE
(MANDARIN)

DICTIONARY &
PHRASEBOOK

Yong Ho

Hippocrene Books, Inc.

New York

ISBN 0-7818-1135-X

Publisher: George Blagowidow
Editor: Robert Stanley Martin
Mandarin copyeditor: Michelle Mei S. Tang
Typesetting: Yong Ho
Cover design: Cynthia Mallard, Cynergie Studio,
                Raleigh, NC

For information, please address:

Hippocrene Books, Inc.
171 Madison Avenue
New York, NY 10016
www.hippocrenebooks.com

*Cataloging-in-Publication data available from the
Library of Congress.*

Printed in the United States of America.

TABLE OF CONTENTS

TABLE OF CONTENTS

QUOTABLE QUOTES

If the 19th century belonged to Britain, and the 20th century to the United States. Then the 21st century will surely belong to China. My advice: Make sure your kids learn Chinese.

Jim Rogers, *Worth Magazine*

The rise of China comes with a whole set of challenges. But the ability to talk to and understand each other should not be among them.

Senator Joseph I. Lieberman

Languages are greatly needed to compete in this world-is-flat society. We want to give our young people opportunities to advance ... and Chinese is a great opportunity to survive in today's economy.

I think there will be two languages in this world. There will be Chinese and English.

Mayor Richard Daley of Chicago

Chinese is strategic in a way that a lot of other languages aren't because of China's growth as an economic and military force.

Scott McGinnis, the Defense Language Institute

As the relationship between China and the United States grows in importance -- a relationship that will dominate the 21st century -- so grows the importance of having our children learn the Chinese language. At China Institute, we believe that "The Future Speaks Chinese."

Sara McCalpin, China Institute

There is more awareness of how important China is. If you are going into business, China may be a source of suppliers or consumers. If I were going to be an economist, I would think studying Chinese would be an extremely interesting investment to make.

Haun Saussy, Yale University

In the next decade the new "must learn" language is likely to be Mandarin

David Graddol, *Journal of Science*

从开封到纽约—辉煌如过眼烟云

As the Chinese headline above puts it, in a language of the future that many more Americans should start learning, "glory is as ephemeral as smoke and clouds."

Nicholas D. Kristof, *New York Times*

雄心勃勃，实力雄厚，烦躁不安，准备迎
接，中国世纪

*If you can't read these words, better start
brushing up. A profound shift has begun, the
kind that occurs once every few lifetimes. Don't
be left behind.*

On Oct. 23, 2004, these were the ominous words
emblazoned on the cover of Canada's *Globe and
Mail*

*Take my advice. Enroll your kids in Mandarin
immersion. One day, they will thank you.*

Margaret Wente, *Globe and Mail*

*Language is a look in. One doesn't need to be
proficient in Chinese languages in order to do
business in China. But the exposure and the
motivation to show that one understands and
respects the Chinese culture is really half the
battle won.*

Michael Levine, *Asia Society*

INTRODUCTION

The renowned travel guru Arthur Frommer recently said in *Newsweek*, "China is now a major travel destination. It is a country that every American needs to see, to glimpse the role that China will play as the 21st century unfolds." *National Geography* listed ten cities that one must visit in his or her lifetime and two of them are in China (Hong Kong and Beijing/Great Wall). The London-based *Knight Ridder/Tribune Business News* predicts that by 2007 China will replace the United States as the largest originator of world tourists. With the ascension of China on the political and economic stage of the world, it is expected that more and more tourists and businesspeople will travel to China. It is with these people in mind that this book is prepared. The ability to speak Chinese is not a prerequisite for traveling to China, as English is spoken in tourist hotels and by tour guides. English is the first foreign language in China, so you won't have trouble finding someone who can speak English. However, some knowledge of Chinese will go a long way toward making your life easier, winning you friends and tiding you over emergencies. Your ability to speak Chinese, however modest it may be, will be tremendously appreciated by Chinese people you come into contact with.

Many people who have traveled to China fall in love with the country and become fascinated by its people and culture, an interest they may entertain for years to come. For these people, I would suggest serious study of Chinese that would certainly go beyond this book. When I wrote my *Beginners Chinese* in 1997 (also by Hippocrene), I quoted the economist Jim Rogers as saying "If the 19th century belonged to Britain, and the 20th century to the United States. Then the 21st century will surely belong to China. My advice: Make sure your kids learn Chinese." Since then, I've seen many people take the plunge themselves instead of waiting for their kids. I congratulate those who have taken up the challenge, as they have made a very wise decision. There are many compelling reasons for people to learn Chinese: it is the most spoken tongue in the world; it is one of the six official languages of the United Nations; and it is the second largest foreign language in the United States. As I'm writing, a headline just appeared in *New York Times* that reads, "Classes in Chinese Grow as the Language Rides a Wave of Popularity." If these are still not enough, see if the quotes in the previous pages can persuade you. Learning Chinese to any extent is a worthwhile investment to make.

So, armed with the language you have learned, go on your trip to unlock the best of China!

6

Terms

There are a few terms that need to be clarified and explained on the outset. These are:

中国 ZHŌNGGUÓ

This is Chinese for *China*, which literally means *middle kingdom*.

中文 ZHŌNGWÉN & 汉语 HÀNYǓ

Both of these two terms refer to the Chinese language. The term 汉语 hànyǔ, which is widely used in China and adopted as the title for most Chinese language textbooks, literally means "the language of the *Han*". *Han* is the second imperial dynasty of China (206 BC-220 AD). Due to its importance in history, the name *Han* came to be used to refer to the ethnic Chinese. It is not difficult to see that 汉语 hànyǔ is not a politically correct term to use, because Chinese is also spoken by most of the minority groups in China as the second language and some of them as the first language. For this reason, 中文 zhōngwén would be a better term. It simply means the language of China.

国语 GUÓYǓ & 普通话 PǓTŌNGHUÀ

Both of these two terms refer to Mandarin. Mandarin is a major dialect of Chinese. It is spoken by over 900 million or 70% of the Chinese people in northern and parts of southern China, but more importantly, it is understood by 94% of the population. The standard Mandarin is based on, but not equivalent to, the Beijing dialect. The term 国语 guóyǔ, which means "national language," is used in Taiwan, Hong Kong and overseas Chinese communities and the term 普通话 pǔtōnghuà, which means "common speech," is used in mainland China. This standard form has become an administrative and official medium. It is used on television, in radio broadcasts and in movies. More importantly, it has been promoted to be the language of instruction in primary and secondary schools. As such, 国语 guóyǔ/普通话 pǔtōnghuà is the prestige form of speech that most people try to emulate.

THE WADE-GILES SYSTEM & THE 拼音 PĪNYĪN SYSTEM

Chinese is not a phonetic language and the written script of Chinese does not bear any resemblance to the actual pronunciation. For this reason, a system of transcribing Chinese phonetics was needed to assist people to learn to read words in Chinese. There are two systems currently in use. One is the Wade-Giles system and the other is the *pinyin* system. The Wade-Giles system was developed by Sir Thomas Francis Wade in the mid-19th century and modified by the Cambridge professor Herbert Allen Giles at the beginning of the last century. This system makes it easier, particularly for English speakers, to pronounce Chinese sounds, but it is not the accurate representation of the sounds. For example, the Wade-Giles system often uses one symbol to represent different sounds and different symbols to represent the same sound. In mainland China, the Wade-Giles system has been replaced by the *pinyin* (which literally means putting sounds together) system which was developed in 1958 with the purpose of introducing standard pronunciation of Mandarin to school children. This system has been practically adopted worldwide since the late 1970s. The *pinyin* system is a more accurate reflection of the actual sounds in Chinese, but you need to know *pinyin* before you can use it. The *pinyin* system is used in this book.

CHINESE PHONETICS

There are 6 vowels (a, o, e, i, u, ü) and 21 consonants (b, p, m, f, d, t, n, l, g, k, h, j, q, x, z, c, s, zh, ch, sh, r) in Mandarin Chinese.

The syllabic structure in Chinese—the ways in which sounds are combined to form syllables—takes the following forms:

V—a vowel standing by itself, such as a, i, u.

VV or VVV—two or three vowels can be combined to form a compound vowel, such as: ao, ai, ou, ei, ia, iao, ie, iu, ua, uo, ue, ui, uai.

CV (CVV, CVVV)—a consonant plus one or more vowels such as ni, hao and piao.

CVC—a consonant plus a vowel plus a consonant, but the final C can only be the nasal sounds -n and –ng, and the retroflex -r, such as jing, nan and er.

Consonant clusters—two or more consonants used in succession—are not permitted in Chinese.

It is not difficult to see from the above that there is a poverty of possible sound

10

combinations in Chinese to express all the meanings that we have. A simple math will tell us that there are only about 400 possible sound combinations in Chinese. The result of this poverty is the proliferation of homophones, words that are pronounced the same but mean differently, because a single sound combination is called upon to express many different meanings. This is not convenient or effective. To alleviate this problem, Chinese resorts to a variety of means, chief among them being the use of four tones. By introducing four tones, the total number of possible sound combinations is quickly boosted to around 1,600. It is still not enough, but it is a tremendous relief.

There is a bright side to this hindrance to effective communication. That is, foreign students of Chinese don't have to learn too many sound combinations. Once they have learned all the possible sound combinations together with the tones, there are no further sound combinations to learn. The total number of possible sound combinations can be plotted on one page only. This can be found in my *Beginners Chinese*.

TONES

As mentioned above, tones are an effective means to reduce homophones and, consequently, ambiguity. Tones are variations of pitch contours. Such variations also occur in English, but they do not change the lexical or basic meaning of the word. In Mandarin, however, pitch changes distinguish meanings. By varying the pitch of a sound combination, you get a totally different word. Here are some examples:

mā (mother), má (hemp), mǎ (horse), mà (scold)
yī (one), yí (move), yǐ (chair), yì (hundred million)
wū (house), wú (none), wǔ (five), wù (fog)

In Mandarin Chinese, there are four tones, which are referred to as the first tone, the second tone, the third tone and the fourth tone, and are respectively indicated by the tone graphs in the following sound combinations: mā, má, mǎ, mà. The workings of these four tones are demonstrated by the following chart.

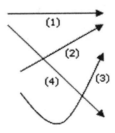

The first tone is called the high level tone. As the name suggests, it should be high, almost at the upper limit of your pitch range, and level, without any fluctuation.

The second tone is called the rising tone. It starts from the middle of your pitch range and rises.

The third tone is called the falling-rising tone. As such, it has two parts: first falling, and then rising. It moves down from the lower half of the pitch range and moves up to a point near the top.

The fourth tone is called the falling tone. It falls precipitously all the way down from the top of the pitch level.

In addition to the four tones, Mandarin Chinese has a "fifth" tone, which is actually a toneless tone. As such it is usually called the neutral tone. Its pronunciation is soft and quick. The neutral tone is not diacritically marked. It occurs with either grammatical particles or the second character of some words that do not receive stress.

PRONUNCIATION GUIDE

Pinyin	Approximate English Equivalent
a	as in father
ao	as in now
ai	as in eye
an	as in man
ang	as in hung
o	as in lore
ou	as in tow
ong	as own
e	as in nurse
ei	as in make
en	as in under
eng	as in sung
er	as in err
i	as in meet
i (after z, c, s, zh, ch, sh and r)	(silent)
ia	as in yacht
iao	as in meow
ian	as in yen
iang	as in young
iong	as in German jünger
ie	as in yes
in	as in yoke
ing	as in pin

ing	as in p**ing**
u	as in r**u**de
ua	as in **wa**ddle
uo	as in **wa**ll
uai	as in **wai**t
uan	as in **wan**d
uang	as in **oo**+**hung**
ui	as in **weigh**
un	as in **wen**t
ü	as in French t**u**
üan	as in **ü**+**an**
üe	as in **ü**+**eh**
ün	as in German gr**ün**
b	as in **b**at
p	as in **p**at
m	as in **m**ap
f	as in **f**at
d	as in **d**a**d**
t	as in **t**ake
n	as in **n**ight
l	as in **l**et
g	as in **g**o
k	as in **k**ey
h	as in **h**op
j	as in **j**ump

PRONUNCIATION GUIDE

q	as in **ch**eese
x	as in **sh**eep
z	as in pi**z**za
c	as in ha**ts**
s	as in **s**and
zh	as in rou**ge**
ch	as in **ch**arge
sh	as in **sh**arp
r	as in **r**ay

A BRIEF CHINESE GRAMMAR

Chinese is not an inflectional language. Words are invariable, unaltered and allow no internal changes. Affixes signaling lexical or grammatical meanings exist, but they do not figure very large in the language. Syntactic and lexical meanings are not indicated through the manipulation of word forms, but through word order, specific particles and vocabulary items. This is a boon for foreign students of Chinese as they do not have to memorize any conjugation tables and inflectional rules.

PARTS OF SPEECH

Parts of speech in Chinese are difficult to define because of the lack of inflectional markers. Most words gain their parts of speech in the context of a phrase or sentence. For this reason, most Chinese dictionaries refrain from indicating the parts of speech of words. Parts of speech are indicated in the dictionary section of this book primarily for the convenience of readers. They are mainly based on the frequency with which they appear syntactically in everyday language.

NOUNS

Chinese does not make distinctions in number. In other words, nouns are not marked to show singular or plural. For example:

我 有 一 本 书。
Wǒ yǒu yì běn shū.
I have one book.

我 有 两 本 书。
Wǒ yǒu liǎng běn shū.
I have two book. (literal translation)

我 有 很 多 书。
Wǒ yǒu hěn duō shū.
I have many book. (literal translation)

In 我有哥哥 wǒ yǒu gēge (I have old brother(s), *literal translation*), this 哥哥 gēge can be either single or plural.

Chinese does not make distinctions in case either. There is no opposition between *I* and *me*, *he* and *him*, *she* and *her*, *we* and *us*, and *they* and *them*.

Chinese does not have articles such as *a, an* and *the* in English. The definiteness and indefiniteness are mainly indicated by word order. Generally, definite items appear at the beginning of a sentence, while indefinite items appear toward the end of the sentence. Contrast:

厕所　在 哪儿?

Cèsuǒ zài nǎr?

Where is the bathroom? (厕所cèsuǒ
[bathroom] is particular.)

哪儿有　厕所?

Nǎr yǒu cèsuǒ?

Where can I find a bathroom? (厕所cèsuǒ
[bathroom] is unspecified)

客人 来 了。

Kèrén lái le.

The guests have come. (客人 kèrén [guests]
are expected.)

来 了 客人。

Lǎi le kèrén.

There came guests. (客人 kèrén [guests] are
unexpected.)

ADJECTIVES

Adjectives in Chinese can function as
predicates without a linking verb such as the
English *be* (see Predicative Adjective in the
Grammatical Terms section). For this reason,
adjectives in Chinese can be considered quasi-
verbs. When used as predicates, adjectives
usually need to be modified by an adverb
instead of standing by themselves:

今天　天气　很　冷。
Jīntiān tiānqì hěn lěng.
It is quite cold today.

你的 中文　　非常　　好。
Nǐde Zhōngwén fēicháng hǎo.
Your Chinese is very good.

The other type of adjectives is attributive adjectives. They are the adjectives that are used before nouns. In Chinese, a monosyllabic adjective can directly modify a noun:

好　人
hǎo rén
good person

旧 车
jiù chē
old car

But 的 de is needed when the adjective is disyllabic or polysyllabic:

高兴　　的 事
gāoxìng de shì
happy event

有意思 的 电影
yǒuyìsi de diànyǐng
interesting movie

A monosyllabic attributive adjective modified by an adverb also requires the use of 的 de before a noun:

很 好 的 人
hěn hǎo de rén
very good person

非常　热 的 夏天
fēicháng rè de xiàtiān
extremely hot summer

Adjectives in the dictionary section of this book mostly have a 的 de after them, but 的 de is dropped when the adjective is used predicatively.

VERBS

Chinese does not distinguish between first/second person and third person (such as *I speak* vs. *he speaks*), between active voice and passive voice (such as *call* vs. *be called*) and between conditional sentences and subjunctive mood (such as *if you are not coming, I'm not going* and *if I had known, I would have done it*).

Tense is conspicuously absent in Chinese. The concept of tense has two components: time (past, present, future, etc.) and aspect (manner of the action). Fortunately for students of

Chinese, verbs do not present a major problem as time is expressed lexically and aspect makers are few and far between in Chinese. There are only three aspects distinguished in Chinese: indefinite, complete and continuous.

The indefinite aspect is not grammatically marked.

The complete or perfective aspect is indicated by the particle 了 le, as in:

火车　到　了。
Huǒchē dào le.
The train has arrived.

他 去了 中国。
Tā qù le Zhōngguó.
He has gone to China.

Although completed actions are usually in the past, they can be in the future as well, such as the English "By the end of the week I will have finished reading the book." For example:

我 下 了 班　就 回　家。
Wǒ xià le bān jiù huí jiā.
I'll go home as soon as I get off work.

The continuous aspect is indicated by the particle 在 zài before the verb:

我 在 看书。
Wǒ zài kànshū.
I'm reading.

他 在 打 电话。
Tā zài dǎ diànhuà.
He is making a phone call.

Again this makes no reference to time. The above two sentences could also be cast in the past in the same form when there is a time indicator:

我 昨天 晚上 九点 在
Wǒ zuótiān wǎnshang jiǔ diǎn zài
看书。
kànshū.
I was reading at 9 last night.

你 来 的 时候，他 在 打 电话。
Nǐ lái de shíhou, tā zài dǎ diànhuà.
When you came, he was making a phone call.

CLASSIFIERS

Classifiers are a category of words that are unique to Chinese and most other Sino-Tibetan languages to which Chinese belongs. Basically, a classifier is a word that comes in between a number or a demonstrative pronoun (e.g. *this*, *that*) and a noun. They are occasionally used in English such as "a *piece* of paper," "a *school* of fish" and "two *heads* of cauliflower", but in Chinese the use of classifiers is the rule rather than the exception. What the classifiers do is to help disambiguate homophones and supply additional semantic information about the nouns they are used with. A particular classifier is usually shared by a number of nouns having the same underlying semantic features. The most commonly used classifiers in Chinese amount to probably less than twenty. The following is a list of the most frequently used classifiers in Chinese:

Classifiers	Semantic Features	Examples
把 bǎ	objects with a handle	knife, umbrella, toothbrush, chair, flag, spade, scissors
本 běn	bound printed material	books, magazines, atlas, album
个 ge	piece; entity	person, bank, shelf, nail, school
件 jiàn	articles (of furniture, luggage, etc.); upper body clothing	shirt, coat, jacket, sweater, luggage, furniture

块 kuài	cube-like objects	soap, cake, watch, brick, block
辆 liàng	vehicles	car, bicycle, motorcycle, truck, carriage
条 tiáo	belt-like and long objects; lower body clothing	towel, fish, street, river, banner, scarf, tie, snake, belt, pants, shorts, skirt
位 wèi	respectable person	teacher, guest, friend, doctor, customer
张 zhāng	flat, rectangular objects	map, bed, table, desk, paper
枝 zhī	long and thin objects	pencil, cigarette, rifle
只 zhī	animals; one of paired items	butterfly, cat, chicken, hand, leg, chopstick, glove, sock
座 zuò	large, solid structure	mountain, bridge, building

Whenever you are stuck with any classifier, use 个 ge instead. This is because 个 ge is the most frequently used classifier in Chinese. It is used for people and most objects. Chances are the classifier that you are stuck for is 个 ge anyway.

WAYS TO ASK QUESTIONS

Yes/No questions

Yes/no questions are questions that require either a *yes* answer or a *no* answer. Chinese does not switch around sentence constituents to form a yes/no question. Rather, it indicates the question by adding the sentence final particle 吗 (ma) at the end of the declarative sentence. For example:

你 好 吗?
Nǐ hǎo ma?
How are you? (literally, *are you good*?)

你 爸爸 忙 吗?
Nǐ bàba máng ma?
Is your father busy?

你 说 中文 吗?
Nǐ shuō Zhōngwén ma?
Do you speak Chinese?

In responding, there is no equivalent in Chinese to *yes* or *no* in English. In other words, there is not a single specific word that we can use all the time to respond to various yes/no questions. Equivalents to *yes* and *no* are actually the verbs or predicative adjectives in the questions. For this reason, they vary from sentence to sentence. Consider the following questions in English:

> 1. Do you speak Chinese?
> 2. Do you like Japanese food?
> 3. Are you a doctor?
> 4. Can you cook?

All you need to do is to answer by using the verb or the verb-like adjective. Positive and negative answers to the above questions would be:

> 1. Speak/not speak.
> 2. Like/not like.
> 3. Am/am not.
> 4. Can/cannot.

In answering a yes/no question in Chinese, you can practically drop everything in the sentence including the subject except the verb or the verb-like adjective.

In addition to the use of the sentence-final particle 吗 ma, yes/no questions can also be indicated by repeating the verb/adjective using its negative form (affirmative + negative). For example:

你 工 作　不 工 作 ?
Nǐ gōngzuò bu gōngzuò?
Do you work?

他 是 不 是 中国人?
Tā shì bu shì Zhōngguórén?
Is he Chinese?

Wh-questions

The term *wh-question* is borrowed from English grammar to refer to those questions that require specific answers instead of yes-no ones. *Wh*-questions include *who, whose, what, which, when, where, why* and *how*. Contrary to English where these interrogative words are placed at the beginning of the questions, Chinese does not change their placement in the sentence, thus *what is this* in English would be *this is what* in Chinese, and *what do you like to eat* in English would be *you like to eat what* in Chinese. The status of the sentence as a question is indicated not by placing the question word at the beginning of the sentence, but simply by the presence of this interrogative word in the sentence. This syntactic feature actually makes it easier for nonnative speakers of Chinese. When asked a *wh*-question, you just need to address the question word, while keeping everything else intact. There is no need to move sentence constituents around. For example:

你 看 什么?
Nǐ kàn shénme?
What are you reading?

我 看 书。
Wǒ kàn shū.
I'm reading a book.

你 在 哪儿工作?
Nǐ zài nǎr gōngzuò?
Where do you work?

我 在 学校 工作。
Wǒ zài xuéxiào gōngzuò.
I work in a school?

The following is a complete list of *Wh-*
question words in Chinese:

什么 shénme (what)
谁 shéi/shuí (who)
谁的 shéide/shuíde (whose)
哪 nǎ (which)
哪儿 nǎr/哪里 nǎlǐ/什么地方 shénme dìfang
(where)
什么时候 shénme shíhou (when)
什么时间/几点 shénme shíjiān/jǐ diǎn (what
time)
为什么 wèi shénme (why)
怎么 zěnme (how)

Alternative question
The alternative question asks for a choice
between two items. It is formed by using 还是
(háishi, meaning *or*) between two choices, e.g.

你 喜欢　吃 中国饭　　　还是 日本饭？
Nǐ xǐhuan chī Zhōngguófàn háishi Rìběnfàn?
Do you like Chinese food or Japanese food?

厕所 在　三 楼 还是 四楼？
Cèsuǒ zài sān lóu háishi sì lóu?
Is the bathroom on the third floor or the fourth floor?

Word order

The basic word order in Chinese is SVO: Subject + Verb + Object. As mentioned earlier, word order plays a role of paramount importance in Chinese. There are three cardinal principles that govern the word order in Chinese.

<u>The principle of modifiers preceding modified</u>

Modifiers in Chinese are always placed before what is modified, whether they are words, phrases or sentences. Chinese is much more consistent than English in this regard. Take the noun modifiers for example. With few exceptions, single-word modifiers of nouns would precede nouns such as "the Bush Doctrine" and "*interesting* story" in English, but as soon as the modifier gets above the phrase level, it immediately follows the noun instead of preceding it. See the following diagram for the contrast:

Chinese

Modifier	*precedes*	Modified

Noun	
Adjective	
Prepositional phrase	Noun
Verb	
Sentence	

Adverb	Adjective
Adverb	Adverb
Adverb	Verb

English

Modified	*precedes*	Modifier

Noun	Prep. phrase
Noun	Clause
Verb	Adverb
Verb	Clause

Once this principle is understood, it will be easy to understand why time, place and manner expressions precede the verbs instead of following them as is the case in English.

The principle of temporal sequence
Briefly stated, this means what happens earlier in time and what exists earlier in conception comes earlier in the sentence. This is a

33

phenomenon referred to by linguists as iconicity. See, for example:

从　　纽约　开车　到 旧金山　要
Cóng Niǔyuē kāichē dào Jiùjīnshān yào
　1　　　　2　　　3

多少时间？
duōshao shíjiān?
How long does it take to drive from New York to San Francisco?

The logical and temporal sequence is: from New York—drive—to San Francisco.

This also explains why in Chinese the first sentence below is much more natural than the second:

认识你，我 很　高兴。
Rěshi nǐ, wǒ hěn gāoxìng.
To know you, I'm very happy.

我 很　高兴，　认识 你。
Wǒ hěn gāoxìng, rènshi nǐ.
I'm very happy to know you.

This is because "to know you" is the cause of "I'm happy."

<u>The principle of whole preceding part</u>
This refers to a regularity in Chinese where a sentence constituent that commands a larger

scope precedes a sentence constituent that commands a smaller scope. This is the exact reverse of English, where the reverse is true. The classic examples are the way we address an envelope in Chinese starting from the largest geographic unit and the way we express time concepts such as 2006 年 5 月 3 日上午 9 点, as opposed to 9 o'clock on the morning of May 3, 2006. This principle also explains the relative positions of elements in the following sentences (double underlining stands for whole, whereas single underlining stands for part):

中国城　　　哪 家 餐馆　　最 好？
Zhōngguóchéng nǎ jiā cānguǎn zuì hǎo?
Which restaurant in Chinatown is the best?

米饭 和 面条，　你 喜欢　哪 个？
Mǐfàn hé miàntiáo, nǐ xǐhuān nǎ ge?
Which do you prefer, rice or noodles?

我们班　　大多数　学生　　　是
Wǒmen bān dà duōshù xuéshēng shì
外国人。
wàiguórén.
Most students in our class are foreign.

这 些 电影　我 多半　都 看 过。
Zhè xiē diànyǐng wǒ duōbàn dōu kàn guo.
I've seen most of these movies.

GRAMMATICAL TERMS EXPLAINED

ADVERBIAL

A word, phrase or clause that modifies a verb, an adjective or another adverb, providing such information as time, place, manner, reason, condition and so on.

ASPECT

The manner in which an action takes place. English distinguishes four aspects: indefinite, continuous, perfect and perfect continuous, whereas Chinese distinguishes indefinite, continuous and perfect. The indefinite aspect indicates the habitual or repeated action. The continuous aspect indicates the continuation or progression of the action. The perfect aspect indicates the completion of an action.

CLASSIFIER

A word used between a numeral and a noun to show a sub-class to which the noun belongs.

COMPLEMENT

The part of the sentence that follows the verb and completes the verb. As such, they are also called verb complements. The most common complements in Chinese are those of direction, result and degree. Directional complements indicate the direction of the action in relation to the speaker and are not separated from the verb by any particle. Complements of result and degree indicate the result and the degree of the action expressed by the verb, and they are separated from the verb by the particle 得 de.

OBJECT

A noun, pronoun, phrase or clause that is used after, and affected in some way by, a transitive verb. If it is affected in a direct way, it is called the direct object. If it is affected in an indirect way, it is called the indirect object. In the sentence *he gave me a book*, *a book* is the direct object and *me* is the indirect object.

PARTICLE

A word that has only grammatical meaning, but no lexical meaning, such as 吗 ma, 呢 ne and 吧 ba in Chinese.

PREDICATE

The part of a sentence that states or asserts something about the subject. This role is only assumed by the verb in English, but can also be assumed by the adjective in Chinese.

PREDICATIVE ADJECTIVE

An adjective used after the verb *to be* in English, as in *the book is <u>interesting</u>*, which is opposed to an attributive adjective used before a noun, as in *this is an <u>interesting</u> book*. The predicative adjective in Chinese is used without the verb *to be*, and functions as the predicate of the sentence.

SUBJECT

Something about which a statement or assertion is made in the rest of the sentence.

TRANSITIVE & INTRANSITIVE VERBS

A transitive verb is one that needs to take an object such as we study Chinese. An intransitive verb is one that does not take an object such as walk, run and go.

ABBREVIATIONS & CONVENTIONS

adjective	adj.
adverb	adv.
article	art.
auxiliary verb	aux.
conjunction	conj.
interjection	interj.
noun	n.
preposition	prep.
pronoun	pron.
question word	ques.
verb	v.
expression	exp.
honorific	hon.
idiom	id.
somebody	sb.
something	sth.

The underlined items in the phrasebook are accompanied by substitutable words.

CHINESE-ENGLISH DICTIONARY

A

ā 啊 (interj.) oh

ài 爱 (n., v.) love

ǎi 矮 (adj.) short (in height)

āidào 哀悼 (n.) condolences

áizhèng 癌症 (n.) cancer

Ālābórén 阿拉伯人 (n.) Arab

Ālābóyǔ 阿拉伯语 (n.) Arabic

ānjìngde 安静的 (adj.) quiet

ānquánde 安全的 (adj.) safe

áoyè 熬夜 (v.) stay up

āyí 阿姨 (n.) aunt

āsīpīlín 阿司匹林 (n.) aspirin

B

bǎi 百 (n.) hundred

báisède 白色的 (adj.) white

bǎiwàn 百万 (n.) million

bāléiwǔ 芭蕾舞 (n.) ballet

bān 搬 (v.) move (into a new home)

bànfǎ 办法 (n.) way, method

bāng 帮 (v.) help

bàngōngshì 办公室 (n.) office

bàngqiú 棒球 (n.) baseball

bāngzhù 帮助 (n., v.) help

bānjí 班级 (n.) class

bànzhíde 半职的 (adj.) part-time

bāo 包 (n., v.) bag; wrap (up)

bǎochí 保持 (v.) keep, maintain

bǎocún 保存 (v.) conserve

bǎode 饱的 (adj.) full (cannot eat anymore)

bàogào 报告 (n., v.) report

bāoguǒ 包裹 (n.) package, parcel

bāohán 包含 (v.) contain

bāokuò 包括 (v.) include

bǎomǔ 保姆 (n.) baby-sitter

bàoqiàn 抱歉 (adj.) sorry

bǎotǎ 宝塔 (n.) pagoda

bàoyuàn 抱怨 (v.) complain

bǎozhèng 保证 (n., v.) guarantee

bàozhǐ 报纸 (n.) newspaper

Bāxī 巴西 (n.) Brazil

Bāxīrén 巴西人 (n.) Brazilian

bāxīde 巴西的 (adj.) Brazilian

bāyuè 八月 (n.) August

bèibāo 背包 (n.) backpack, knapsack

bèidān 被单 (n.) sheet (bed)

běifāng 北方 (n.) north

běifāngde 北方的 (adj.) northern

běifāngrén 北方人 (n.) northerner

bèiléimào 贝雷帽 (n.) beret

bēishāngde 悲伤的 (adj.) sad

bèitòng 背痛 (n.) backache

bèixīn 背心 (n.) vest

bèizi 被子 (n.) comforter

bēizi 杯子 (n.) cup, glass

bēizi 杯子 (n.) glass (drinking)

bēngdài 绷带 (n.) bandage

bēngkuì 崩溃 (v.) crumble

bǐ...dà 比…大 (exp.) older than

bǐ...xiǎo 比…小 (exp.) younger than

biān 边 (n.) side

biānjí 编辑 (n.) editor

biànjí 遍及 (prep.) throughout

biānjìe 边界 (n.) border

biànhuà 变化 (n., v.) change

biànmì 便秘 (n.) constipation

biǎoshì 表示 (v.) show, indicate

biǎoxiàn 表现 (v.) behave

biǎoyǎn 表演 (n., v.) performance; perform

biéde 别的 (adj.) other

bǐjiào 比较 (n., v.) comparison; compare

bǐjìběn 笔记本 (n.) notebook

Bǐlìshí 比利时 (n.) Belgium

Bǐlìshírén 比利时人 (n.) Belgian

bìmiǎn 避免 (v.) avoid

bì'nànsuǒ 避难所 (n.) asylum

bīng 冰 (n.) ice

bīngqílín 冰淇淋 (n.) ice cream

bīngxiāng 冰箱 (n.) refrigerator

bìránde 必然的 (adj.) certain

bǐsài 比赛 (n., v.) competition; compete

bìxū 必须 (aux.) must

bìyàode 必要的 (adj.) necessary

bìyè 毕业 (n., v.) graduation; graduate

bìyùn yòngjù 避孕用具 (n.) contraceptive

bìyùntào 避孕套 (n.) condom

bìyùnwán 避孕丸 (n.) birth control pill

bízi 鼻子 (n.) nose

bō 剥 (v.) peel

bóshì 博士 (n.) Ph.D.

bówùguǎn 博物馆 (n.) museum

bù 布 (n.) cloth

bù 部 (n.) ministry (government)

bù 不 (adv.) no

bùxúnchángde 不寻常的 (adj.) unusual

bù 布 (n.) fabric

búbiànde 不便的 (adj.) inconvenient

bǔcháng 补偿 (v.) compensate

bùfen 部分 (n.) part

bùjiǔ 不久 (adv.) soon (as soon as possible)

bùkěnéngde 不可能的 (adj.) impossible

bùliào 布料 (n.) material, fabric

bùtóngde 不同的 (adj.) different

bùxíng 步行 (v.) walk (go on foot)

búxìngde 不幸的 (adj.) unfortunate

búzài 不再 (adv.) no more

C

cài 菜 (n.) dish (of food)

cāicè 猜测 (n., v.) guess

càidān 菜单 (n.) menu

cǎifǎng 采访 (n., v.) interview

cáifeng 裁缝 (n.) tailor

cǎi'nà 采纳 (v.) adopt

càipǔ 菜谱 (n.) recipe

cáiwù 财物 (n.) belongings

cáizhèng 财政 (n.) finance

cānguǎn 餐馆 (n.) restaurant

cānjiā 参加 (v.) participate, join, attend

cānjīnzhǐ 餐巾纸 (n.) napkin

cānzhuō 餐桌 (n.) dining table

cāozáde 嘈杂的 (adj.) noisy

cāshǒuzhǐ 擦手纸 (n.) tissue

cèliáng 测量 (v.) measure

céng 层 (n.) floor (in a hotel, etc.)

cèsuǒ 厕所 (n.) bathroom

chá 茶 (n.) tea

cháng 尝 (v.) taste

chàng 唱 (v.) sing

chángcháng 常常 (adv.) often

chángde 长的 (adj.) long

chángdèng 长凳 (n.) bench

chángdù 长度 (n.) length

chǎnghé 场合 (n.) occasion

chángshì 尝试 (n., v.) attempt

chāoshì 超市 (n.) supermarket

cháoshīde 潮湿的 (adj.) wet

chāxiāo 插销 (n.) bolt

chāzi 叉子 (n.) fork

chéng 乘 (v.) take (bus, train, etc.)

chéngběn 成本 (n.) cost

chénggōngde 成功的 (adj.) successful

chéngjiù 成就 (n.) achievement

chéngkè 乘客 (n.) passenger

chéngrén 成人 (n.) adult

chéngrèn 承认 (v.) admit

chéngsè 橙色 (n.) orange (color)

chéngshì 城市 (n.) city

chéngshíde 诚实的 (adj.) honest

chéngwéi 成为 (v.) become

chéngyuán 成员 (n.) member

chēngzàn 称赞 (n., v.) compliment

chéngzhèn 城镇 (n.) town

chéngzhī 橙汁 (n.) orange juice

chènshān 衬衫 (n.) shirt, blouse

chēxiāng 车厢 (n.) compartment

chī 吃 (v.) eat

chǐcùn 尺寸 (n.) size

chíde 迟的 (adj.) late

chìjiǎo 赤脚 (adv.) barefoot

chìluǒde 赤裸的 (adj.) bare

chítáng 池塘 (n.) pond

chóngfù 重复 (v.) repeat

chōngtū 冲突 (n., v.) conflict

chǒulòude 丑陋的 (adj.) ugly

chōuyān 抽烟 (v.) smoke

chú...zhīwài 除…之外 (prep.) besides, except

chuán 船 (n.) boat, ship

chuān 穿 (v.) wear (clothes)

chuānguò 穿过 (v.) cross

chuáng 床 (n.) bed

chuàngzào 创造 (v.) create

chuāngzi 窗子 (n.) window

chuánjiàoshì 传教士 (n.) missionary

chuánrǎnxìngde 传染性的 (adj.) contagious

chuántǒng 传统 (n.) tradition

chuántǒngde 传统的 (adj.) traditional

chuānyī 穿衣 (v.) dress

chuánzhǎng 船长 (n.) captain

chūbǎn 出版 (v.) publish

chúfáng 厨房 (n.) kitchen

chǔfāng 处方 (n.) prescription

chúfēi 除非 (conj.) unless

chuīgān 吹干 (v.) blow-dry

chūjíde 初级的 (adj.) elementary (level)

chuījù 炊具 (n.) cooker

chūkǒu 出口 (n., v.) exit; export

chūmén 出门 (v.) go out

chūntiān 春天 (n.) spring (season)

chūshēng 出生 (v.) be born

chúshī 厨师 (n.) chef, cook

chūxiàn 出现 (n., v.) appearance; appear

chūxuě 出血 (v.) bleed

chūxuézhě 初学者 (n.) beginner, novice

chūzūchē 出租车 (n.) cab, taxi

cí 词 (n.) word

cíhuì 词汇 (n.) vocabulary

cìxiù 刺绣 (n.) embroidery

cǐzhì...jìnglǐ 此致...敬礼 (id.) sincerely yours

cóng 从 (prep.) from

cóngbù 从不 (adv.) never

cónglín 丛林 (n.) jungle

cōngmáng 匆忙 (v.) rush

cōngmíngde 聪明的 (adj.) clever, intelligent, smart

cún 存 (v.) save (money)

cúnkuǎn 存款 (n., v.) deposit

cūnzi 村子 (n.) village

cuòwù 错误 (n.) mistake

cuòwùde 错误的 (adj.) wrong

D

dà 大 (adv.) heavily (regarding rain)

dǎ 打 (v.) beat, hit, strike

dǎ diànhuà 打电话 (id.) call (make a phone call)

dǎ zhāohu 打招呼 (id.) greet

dàdào 大道 (n.) avenue

dàde 大的 (adj.) big, large

dàduōshù 大多数 (n.) majority

dáfù 答复 (n., v.) reply

dài 戴 (v.) wear (a cap or hat)

dài lái 带来 (v.) bring

dàibiǎo 代表 (n., v.) representative; represent

dǎibǔ 逮捕 (n., v.) arrest

dàihào 代号 (n.) code

dàilǐ 代理 (n.) agency

dàilǐshāng 代理商 (n.) agent

dàizi 带子 (n.) belt

dàjiàotáng 大教堂 (n.) cathedral

dàlǐshí 大理石 (n.) marble

dàlù 大陆 (n.) continent

dàn 蛋 (n.) egg

dāng...shí 当...时 (conj.) while, (time) when

dàng'àn wénjiàn 档案文件 (n.) archive

dàn'gāo 蛋糕 (n.) cake

dāngdìde 当地的 (adj.) local

dānshēnde 单身的 (adj.) single (unmarried)

dānshēnhàn 单身汉 (n.) bachelor

dànshì 但是 (conj.) but

dào 倒 (v.) pour

dào 到 (prep., v.) to; arrive

dǎo 岛 (n.) island

dāo 刀 (n.) knife

dàochù 到处 (adv.) everywhere

dàodá 到达 (n., v.) arrival; arrive

dǎogào 祷告 (v.) pray

dàogǔ 稻谷 (n.) paddy

dāopiàn 刀片 (n.) razor

dàoqiàn 道歉 (v.) apologize

dàoqiè 盗窃 (v.) burglarize

dāorèn 刀刃 (n.) blade

dàotián 稻田 (n.) rice paddy

dǎoyǎn 导演 (n.) director (of a movie)

dǎoyóu 导游 (n.) tour guide

dǎrǎo 打扰 (v.) bother

dàshēngde 大声地 (adv.) loudly

dàshēngde 大声的 (adj.) loud

dàshǐ 大使 (n.) ambassador

dàshǐguǎn 大使馆 (n.) embassy

dǎsuàn 打算 (n., v.) plan

dàxué 大学 (n.) university

dàyī 大衣 (n.) coat

dāying 答应 (v.) comply

dǎyìnjī 打印机 (n.) printer (machine)

dàyuē 大约 (prep.) about

de 的 (prep.) of (belonging to)

dédào 得到 (v.) get

děng 等 (v.) wait

dēng 灯 (n.) light, lamp, lantern

dēngjīpái 登机牌 (n.) boarding pass

dēngpào 灯泡 (n.) bulb

diàn 电 (n.) electricity

diǎn 点 (n.) o'clock

diǎn 点 (v.) order (food)

diànchí 电池 (n.) battery

diànhuà 电话 (n.) telephone

diànhuàbù 电话簿 (n.) telephone book

diànhuàkǎ 电话卡 (n.) calling card

diànlǎn 电缆 (n.) cable

diǎnlǐ 典礼 (n.) ceremony

diànnǎo 电脑 (n.) computer

diànshì 电视 (n.) television

diàntī 电梯 (n.) elevator

diànyǐng 电影 (n.) movie

diànyǐngyuàn 电影院 (n.) movie theater

diāoxiàng 雕像 (n.) statue

dìdi 弟弟 (n.) younger brother

dìfāng 地方 (n.) place

dìjiào 地窖 (n.) cellar

dìng 订 (v.) subscribe to, reserve

dìng le hūn de 订了婚的 (adj.) engaged to be married

dìngqīde 定期地 (adv.) regularly

dìqū 地区 (n.) area, region

dāngrán 当然 (adv.) of course

dìtiě 地铁 (n.) subway

dìtú 地图 (n.) map

diū 丢 (v.) lose (sth.)

dìxiàde 地下的 (adj.) underground

dìxiàshì 地下室 (n.) basement

dìyī 第一 (adj.) first

dìzhǐ 地址 (n.) address

dǒng 懂 (v.) understand

dōngfāng 东方 (n.) east

dōngfāngde 东方的 (adj.) eastern

dōngxi 东西 (n.) thing (object)

dǒngshìhuì 董事会 (n.) board

dōngtiān 冬天 (n.) winter

dòngwù 动物 (n.) animal

dòngwùyuán 动物园 (n.) zoo

dòngzuò 动作 (n.) act

dòuhào 逗号 (n.) comma

dòuzi 豆子 (n.) bean

dù 度 (n.) degree (temperature)

dǔ 赌 (n., v.) gamble

dú 读 (v.) read

duìhuàn 兑换 (v.) convert

duǎn 短 (adj.) short (in length)

duǎnkù 短裤 (n.) shorts

duànliàn 锻炼 (v.) work out

duǎnquē 短缺 (n.) shortage

duǎnqún 短裙 (n.) skirt

duǎnwà 短袜 (n.) sock

dǔchǎng 赌场 (n.) casino

duì 队 (n.) queue (line), team

duì 对 (prep.) to, regarding

duìbuqǐ 对不起 (id.) sorry

duìfāng fùfèi diànhuà 对方付费电话 (n.)
    collect call

duìhuà 对话 (n.) dialogue

duìhuànlǜ 兑换率 (n.) rate of exchange

dùjià shèngdì 度假胜地 (n.) resort

dúlì 独立 (n., adj) independence; independent

dúmùzhōu 独木舟 (n.) canoe

dūn 吨 (n.) ton

duō cháng 多长 (ques.) how long

duò 剁 (v.) chop

duòtāi 堕胎 (n.) abortion

dúpǐn 毒品 (n.) drug (as in "drug addiction")

dútède 独特的 (adj.) unique

dúzì 独自 (adv.) alone

dùzi 肚子 (n.) belly

E

èrděng 二等 (adj.) second-class

ěrhuán 耳环 (n.) earring(s)

èrshǒude 二手的 (adj.) used

értóng 儿童 (n.) child, children

èryuè 二月 (n.) February

érzi 儿子 (n.) son

éwàide 额外的 (adj.) additional

F

fābiǎo 发表 (v.) publish

fādòngjī 发动机 (n.) engine

fǎlǜ 法律 (n.) law

fānbùchuáng 帆布床 (n.) cot

fǎnchángde 反常的 (adj.) abnormal

fǎnduì 反对 (prep.) oppose

fàng 放 (v.) place

fāngbiànde 方便的 (adj.) convenient

fángdōng 房东 (n.) landlord

fángjiān 房间 (n.) room

fàngqì 放弃 (v.) abandon

fāngshì 方式 (n.) style, approach

fàngsōng 放松 (v.) relax

fǎngwèn 访问 (n., v.) visit

fāngxiàng 方向 (n.) directions

fángzi 房子 (n.) house

fàn 饭 (n.) meal

fànwǎn 饭碗 (n.) rice bowl

fānyì 翻译 (n., v.) translation (work), translator (person); translate

fànzuì 犯罪 (v.) commit a crime

fāshāo 发烧 (v.) fever

fǎtíng 法庭 (n.) court

fāyīn 发音 (n., v.) pronunciation; pronounce

fāzhǎn 发展 (n., v.) development; develop

fēicháng 非常 (adv.) very much

fēijī 飞机 (n.) airplane

fēijīpiào 飞机票 (n.) plane ticket

fēixíngyuán 飞行员 (n.) pilot

féizào 肥皂 (n.) soap

fēizhèngfǔ zǔzhī 非政府组织 (n.) nongovernmental organization

Fēizhōu 非洲 (n.) Africa

Fēizhōude 非洲的 (adj.) African

Fēizhōurén 非洲人 (n.) African

féng 缝 (v.) sew

fēngbào 风暴 (n.) storm

fēngjǐng 风景 (n.) view, scenery

fēngjǐngdiǎn 风景点 (n.) scenic spot

fēngkuángde 疯狂的 (adj.) crazy

fēngmiàn 封面 (n.) book cover

fēngzheng 风筝 (n.) kite

fěnhóngsède 粉红色的 (adj.) pink

fēnkāide 分开地 (adv.) separately

fènnù 愤怒 (adj.) angry

fēnzhōng 分钟 (n.) minute

Fójiào 佛教 (n.) Buddhism

Fójiàotú 佛教徒 (n.) Buddhist

fùběn 副本 (n.) copy

fùjiàn 附件 (n.) accessory

fúlì 福利 (n.) benefit

fùmǔ 父母 (n.) parents

fūqī 夫妻 (n.) couple (husband and wife)

fùqin 父亲 (n.) father

fúshǒuyǐ 扶手椅 (n.) armchair

fúwù 服务 (n., v.) service; serve

fúwùyuán 服务员 (n.) waiter/waitress

fùxí 复习 (v.) review

fǔyīn 辅音 (n.) consonant

fùyìnjī 复印机 (n.) copy machine

fùzáde 复杂的 (adj.) complicated

G

gǎishàn 改善 (n., v.) improvement; improve

gānbēi! 干杯! (interj.) cheers!

gǎnchē 赶车 (v.) catch a train/bus

gànde 干的 (adj.) dry

gāngbǐ 钢笔 (n.) pen

gānggang 刚刚 (adv.) just now

gǎngkǒu 港口 (n.) port

gǎnjué 感觉 (n., v.) feeling; feel

gǎnmào 感冒 (n.) cold (sickness)

gǎnqíng 感情 (n.) feeling

gānxǐ 干洗 (v.) dry-clean

gāode 高的 (adj.) tall, high

gāo'ěrfūqiú 高尔夫球 (n.) golf

jǐnggào 警告 (v; n.) warning

gàosu 告诉 (v.) tell

gāoxìng 高兴的 (adj.) glad

gāozhōng 高中 (n.) high school

gè 各 (adj.) each

gē 歌 (n.) song

gēge 哥哥 (n.) older brother

gěi 给 (v.) give

gējù 歌剧 (n.) opera

gélóu 阁楼 (n.) attic

gèng duō de 更多的 (adj.) more

gèng huài de 更坏的 (adj.) worse

gèng hǎo de 更好的 (adj.) better

gēngzhèng 更正 (n., v.) correction; correct

gēnjù 根据 (prep.) according to

gēn 跟 (prep.) with

gēnsuí 跟随 (v.) follow

gēshǒu 歌手 (n.) singer

gōng 弓 (n.) bow

gōngchǎng 工厂 (n.) factory

Gōngchǐ 公尺 (n.) meter

gōnggòng qìchē 公共汽车 (n.) bus

gōngjiàng 工匠 (n.) craftsman

gōngjiāo chēzhàn 公交车站 (n.) bus station

gōngjīn 公斤 (n.) kilogram

gōngkāide 公开的 (adj.) public

gōnglǐ 公里 (n.) kilometer

gōnglì 公立 (n.) public

gōngmín 公民 (n.) citizen

gōngshēng 公升 (n.) liter

gōngsī 公司 (n.) company

gòngtóngde 共同的 (adj.) common

gōngyè 工业(n.) industry

gōngyì 工艺 (n.) craft

gōngyù 公寓 (n.) apartment

gōngyuán 公园 (n.) park

gōngzī 工资 (n.) salary

gōngzuò 工作 (n., v.) job; work

gǒu 狗 (n.) dog

gòuwù 购物 (v.) shop

guā 刮 (v.) shave

guà (diànhuà) 挂 (电话) (v.) hang up (the phone)

guǎfu 寡妇 (n.) widow

guǎizhàng 拐杖 (n.) crutch

guān 关 (v.) close, turn off (a lamp/lights)

guānbìde 关闭的 (adj.) closed

guāncai 棺材 (n.) coffin

guāndiǎn 观点 (n.) viewpoint

guānfu 鳏夫 (n.) widower

guāng 光 (n.) light

guǎnggào 广告 (n.) advertisement

guānguāng 观光 (v.) sightsee

guānguāngkè 观光客 (n.) sightseer

guǎnlǐ 管理 (n., v.) management; manage

guānxì 关系 (n.) relationship

guānxīn 关心 (n., v.) concern; show concern

guànxǐshì 盥洗室 (n.) lavatory

guānyuán 官员 (n.) official

guānfāngde 官方的 (adj.) official

gǔdài 古代 (n.) antiquity, ancient time

gǔdàide 古代的 (adj.) ancient

gǔdiǎnde 古典的 (adj.) classic

guìde 贵的 (adj.) expensive

guīhuán 归还 (v.) return (sth.)

guìtái 柜台 (n.) counter

gùkè 顾客 (n.) customer

gǔlì 鼓励 (n., v.) encouragement; encourage

gūmā 姑妈 (n.) aunt

guòchéng 过程 (n.) course, process

guòdào 过道 (n.) aisle

guójí 国籍 (n.) citizenship

guójì 国际 (adj.) international

guójì xiàngqí 国际象棋 (n.) chess

guójiā 国家 (n.) nation, country, state

guòmǐn 过敏 (adj.) allergic

guòmǐnzhèng 过敏症 (n.) allergy

guòqù 过去 (n.) past

guówài 国外 (adv.) abroad

guǒzhī 果汁 (n.) juice

gùshi 故事 (n.) story

gǔtou 骨头 (n.) bone

gùyuán 雇员 (n.) employee

gǔzhǎng 鼓掌 (v.) applaud

gùzhàng 故障 (n.) breakdown, malfunctioning

H

hái 还 (adv.) yet, still

hǎi 海 (n.) sea

hǎi'àn 海岸 (n.) coast, seashore

hǎibá gāodù 海拔高度 (n.) altitude

hǎiguān 海关 (n.) customs (at an airport)

hǎijūn 海军 (n.) navy (military)

hàipà 害怕 (adj.) afraid

hǎitān 海滩 (n.) beach

hǎiwān 海湾 (n.) bay

hǎiyáng 海洋 (n.) ocean

hǎn 喊 (v.) cry

hàn 汗 (n.) sweat

hángbān 航班 (n.) flight (of planes)

hángkōng gōngsī 航空公司 (n.) airline

hángkōng yóujiàn 航空邮件 (n.) airmail

hǎo 好 (adj., interj.) good; okay

hǎo a 好啊 (id.) all right

hǎochīde 好吃的 (adj.) delicious

hàokède 好客的 (adj.) hospitable

hàoqíde 好奇的 (adj.) curious

hǎoxiàng 好像 (v.) seem

hē 喝 (v.) drink

hé 河 (n.) river

hé 和 (conj.) and

hé'ǎide 和蔼的 (adj.) kind

héhuǒrén 合伙人 (n.) partner

hēi'ànde 黑暗的 (adj.) dark

hēibǎn 黑板 (n.) blackboard

hēisède 黑色的 (adj.) black

hèn 恨 (v.) hate

hěn 很 (adv.) very

hépíng 和平 (n.) peace

hépíngde 和平的 (adj.) peaceful

héshang 和尚 (n.) monk

hétong 合同 (n.) contract

héxīn 核心 (n.) core

hézi 盒子 (n.) box

hēzuìde 喝醉的 (adj.) drunk

hōnggānjī 烘干机 (n.) dryer

hónglǜdēng 红绿灯 (n.) traffic light

hóngsède 红色的 (adj.) red

hòubèi 后背 (n.) back

hòudài 后代 (n.) descendant

hòuguǒ 后果 (n.) consequence

hòulái 后来 (adv.) later, afterward

hú 湖 (n.) lake

huà 画 (n.) painting, picture

huā 花 (n.) flower

huáde 滑的 (adj.) slippery

huàide 坏的 (adj.) bad

huáiyùn 怀孕 (v.) be pregnant

huàjiā 画家 (n.) painter (artist)

huàn 换 (n., v.) change

huánjìng 环境 (n.) circumstance

huángdào 黄道 (n.) zodiac

huángjīn 黄金 (n.) gold

huángsède 黄色的 (adj.) yellow

huǎnmànde 缓慢的 (adj.) slow

huānyíng 欢迎 (n., v.) welcome

huāpíng 花瓶 (n.) vase

huàxué 化学 (n.) chemistry

huàxuéde 化学的 (adj.) chemical

huàxuéjiā 化学家 (n.) chemist

huàxuépǐn 化学品 (n.) chemical

huāyuán 花园 (n.) garden

huí 回 (v.) return (go home)

huī 灰 (n.) ash

huídá 回答 (n., v.) answer

huí diànhuà 回电话 (v.) call back

huìhuà 会话 (n.) conversation

huǐhuài 毁坏 (v.) destroy

huìyì 会议 (n.) conference, meeting

hùnèi 户内 (adv.) indoors

hùnhé 混合 (n., v.) blend

hūnlǐ 婚礼 (n.) wedding

hùnxiáo 混淆 (v.) confuse

huǒ 火 (n.) fire

huòbì 货币 (n.) currency

huǒchái 火柴 (n.) matches

huǒchē 火车 (n.) train

huǒchēzhàn 火车站 (n.) train station

huòdé 获得 (v.) acquire

huódòng 活动 (n.) activity

huóyuède 活跃的 (adj.) active

huózhe 活着 (adj.) alive

huòzhě 或者 (conj.) or

hùshi 护士 (n.) nurse

hùwài 户外 (adv.) outdoors

hūxī 呼吸 (n., v.) breath; breathe

húxū 胡须 (n.) beard

hùzhào 护照 (n.) passport

J

jī 鸡 (n.) chicken

jǐ 几 (ques., adj.) how many, how much; several

jí 急 (adj.) urgent

jiā 加 (v.) add

jiā 家 (n.) home, family

jiàgé 价格 (n.) price

Jiānádà 加拿大 (n.) Canada

Jiānádàde 加拿大的 (adj.) Canadian

Jiānádàrén 加拿大人 (n.) Canadian

jiǎndānde 简单的 (adj.) plain, simple

jiǎndāo 剪刀 (n.) scissors

jiǎnduǎnde 简短的 (adj.) brief

jiāngguǒ 浆果 (n.) berry

jiǎngxuéjīn 奖学金 (n.) scholarship

jiànkāng 健康 (n.) health (of a person)

jiànkāngde 健康的 (adj.) healthy

jiǎnlì 简历 (n.) resume

jiànshè 建设 (n., v.) construction; construct

jiàntóu 箭头 (n.) arrow

jiànyì 建议 (n., v.) suggestion; suggest

jiànzào 建造 (v.) build

jiànzhù 建筑 (n.) architecture, building

jiáo 嚼 (v.) chew

jiāo 教 (v.) teach

jiàocái 教材 (n.) textbook

jiàochē 轿车 (n.) car

jiāodài 胶带 (n.) tape (adhesive tape)

jiāojuǎn 胶卷 (n.) film

jiāojí 焦急 (n.) anxiety

jiāojì 交际 (v.) communicate

jiàokēshū 教科书 (n.) textbook

jiǎoluò 角落 (n.) corner

jiāoqū 郊区 (n.) suburb(s)

jiàoshòu 教授 (n.) professor

jiāotán 交谈 (n.) conversation

jiàotáng 教堂 (n.) church

jiāotōng 交通 (n.) traffic

jiāotōng dǔsè 交通堵塞 (n.) traffic jam

jiāotōng gōngjù 交通工具 (n.) means (of transportation)

jiǎowàn 脚腕 (n.) ankle

jiàoyù 教育 (n., v.) education; educate

jiàqī 假期 (n.) vacation

jiàrì 假日 (n.) holiday

jiāsù 加速 (v.) accelerate

jiātíng 家庭 (n.) family

jíbìng 疾病 (n.) disease

jīchǎng 机场 (n.) airport

jīchǔ 基础 (n.) basis

jìde 记得 (v.) remember

Jīdūjiào 基督教 (n.) Christianity

Jīdūtú 基督徒 (n.) Christian

jiè 借 (v.) borrow, lend

jiē 接 (v.) meet (in order to pick up)

jiē 街 (n.) street

jiēdàiyuán 接待员 (n.) receptionist

jiēdào 街道 (n.) neighborhood

jī'ède 饥饿的 (adj.) hungry

jiéhūn 结婚 (v.) get married

jiějie 姐姐 (n.) older sister

jiémù 节目 (n.) program

jiēnà 接纳 (n.) admission

jiēqū 街区 (n.) block (city block)

jiérì 节日 (n.) festival

jièshào 介绍 (v.) introduce

jiěshì 解释 (n., v.) explanation; explain

jiēshòu 接受 (n., v.) acceptance; accept

jiéshù 结束 (n., v.) end; finish

jiētóu xiǎofàn 街头小贩 (n.) street vendor

jìgōng 技工 (n.) mechanic
jíhé 集合 (v.) assemble
jīhū 几乎 (adv.) almost
jìhuà 计划 (n., v.) plan
jīhuì 机会 (n.) opportunity
jìjié 季节 (n.) season
jìn 近 (adj.) near, close
jǐnde 紧的 (adj.) tight
jīnfàde 金发的 (adj.) blond
jǐngbào 警报 (n.) alarm
jǐngchá 警察 (n.) police officer
jīngjì 经济 (n.) economy
jīngjixué 经济学 (n.) economics
jīnglǐ 经理 (n.) manager
jìngpèi 敬佩 (v.) admire
jīngqí 惊奇 (n.) surprise
jìngzi 镜子 (n.) mirror
jì'niànpǐn 纪念品 (n.) souvenir
jǐnjí qíngkuàng 紧急情况 (n.) emergency
jǐnjíde 紧急的 (adj.) urgent
jìnkǒu 进口 (n., v.) import
jīnróng 金融 (n.) finance
jìnrù 进入 (v.) enter
jǐnshènde 谨慎的 (adj.) cautious
jìnzhǐ 禁止 (n., v.) ban

jīntiān 今天 (n.) today

jìnxǐlǐ 浸洗礼 (n.) baptism

jīnwǎn 今晚 (adv., n.) tonight

jǐnzhāngde 紧张的 (adj.) nervous

jīpiào 机票 (n.) plane ticket

jípǔchē 吉普车 (n.) jeep

jīqì 机器 (n.) machine

jìsù xuéxiào 寄宿学校 (n.) boarding school

jìsuàn 计算 (v.) calculate

jìsuànqì 计算器 (n.) calculator

jítā 吉它 (n.) guitar

jiǔbā 酒吧 (n.) bar

jiùde 旧的 (adj.) old (describing things), used

jiùhùchē 救护车 (n.) ambulance

jiǔjīng 酒精 (n.) alcohol

jiùshēngyī 救生衣 (n.) life jacket

jiǔyuè 九月 (n.) September

jìxù 继续 (v.) continue

jìzhě 记者 (n.) reporter

jǐzhuī 脊椎 (n.) backbone

juǎnchǐ 卷尺 (n.) tape measure

juǎnqū 卷曲 (v.) curl

juédìng 决定 (v., n.) decide; decision

juéduìde 绝对的 (adj.) absolute

juéduìde 绝对地 (adv.) absolutely

jùhuì 聚会 (n., v.) get-together

jūnduì 军队 (n.) army

jūnshìde 军事的 (adj.) military

jǔqǐ 举起 (v.) lift

jùtǐde 具体的 (adj.) concrete

jùzǐ 句子 (n.) sentence (of words)

júzi 桔子 (n.) orange (fruit)

K

kǎchē 卡车 (n.) truck

kāfēi 咖啡 (n.) coffee

kāfēiguǎn 咖啡馆 (n.) café, coffee shop

kāi 开 (v.) turn on (a lamp/lights), drive (a car)

kāihuì 开会 (v.) meet

kāi wánxiào 开玩笑 (v.) joke

kāishǐ 开始 (v., n.) begin, beginning

kàn 看 (v.) look at

kàn diànyǐng 看电影 (v.) go to the movies

kàn yīshēng 看医生 (v.) go to a doctor

kāngkǎide 慷慨的 (adj.) generous

kànjiàn 看见 (v.) see

kǎo 烤 (v.) toast, bake

kǎolǜ 考虑 (v.) consider

kǎoshì 考试 (n.) examination; (v.) take an exam (school)

kǎpiàn 卡片 (n.) cards

kè 课 (n.) lesson

kě'àide 可爱的 (adj.) cute, lovely

kèchéng 课程 (n.) course, subject (school subject)

kèhù 客户 (n.) client

kěkàode 可靠的 (adj.) dependable

kěnéng 可能 (aux.) may

kěnéngde 可能的 (adj.) possible

kěnéngde 可能地 (adv.) possibly

kěpàde 可怕的 (adj.) awful, terrifying

kèrén 客人 (n.) guest

kěrěnshòude 可忍受的 (adj.) bearable, tolerable

késou 咳嗽 (n., v.) cough

kètīng 客厅 (n.) living room

kēxué 科学 (n.) science

kēxuéjiā 科学家 (n.) scientist

kěyǐ 可以 (aux.) can

kèzhàn 客栈 (n.) hostel

kězhuǎnhuànde 可转换的 (adj.) convertible

kòngbáide 空白的 (adj.) blank

kǒngbù zhǔyì 恐怖主义 (n.) terrorism

kōngde 空的 (adj.) empty, vacant

kōngqì 空气 (n.) air

kōngtiáo 空调 (n.) air-conditioning

kòngzhì 控制 (n., v.) control

kǒukěde 口渴的 (adj.) thirsty

kǒuyì 口译 (v.) interpret

kǒuyīn 口音 (n.) accent

kǒuyìyuán 口译员 (n.) interpreter

kū 哭 (v.) cry

kuàide 快的 (adj.) fast

kuàijì 会计 (n.) accountant

kuàilède 快乐的 (adj.) happy

kuàizi 筷子 (n.) chopstick(s)

kuānde 宽的 (adj.) wide

kǔde 苦的 (adj.) bitter

kùn 困 (adj.) sleepy

kùnnánde 困难的 (adj.) difficult

kùzi 裤子 (n.) pants

L

lái 来 (v.) come

lājī 垃圾 (n.) garbage

lāliàn 拉链 (n.) zipper

lǎnduòde 懒惰的 (adj.) lazy

làngmànde 浪漫的 (adj.) romantic

lánqiú 篮球 (n.) basketball

lánsède 蓝色的 (adj.) blue

lánwěiyán 阑尾炎 (n.) appendicitis

lànyòng 滥用 (v.) abuse

lánzi 篮子 (n.) basket

lǎobǎn 老板 (n.) boss

lǎode 老的 (adj.) old (of people)

láodòng 劳动 (n., v.) labor

lǎoshī 老师 (n.) teacher

lǎoshìde 老式的 (adj.) old-fashioned

lǎoshǔ 老鼠 (n.) rat, mouse

làzhú 蜡烛 (n.) candle

lěng 冷 (adj.) cold

lèqù 乐趣 (n.) fun

lèyìde 乐意的 (adj.) ready (willing)

lǐjiě 理解 (v.) understand

liǎn 脸 (n.) face

liángshuǎngde 凉爽的 (adj.) cool

liángxié 凉鞋 (n.) sandal

liǎngzhě 两者 (adj., pron.) both

liánxì 联系 (v.) contact

liànxí 练习 (n.) exercise

liányīqún 连衣裙 (n.) dress

liánzǐ 帘子 (n.) curtain

liànxí 练习 (v., n.) practice; exercise

liànzi 链子 (n.) chain

liáotiān 聊天 (v.) chat

lièfèng 裂缝 (n.) crack

lǐfà 理发 (n.) haircut

lǐfàshī 理发师 (n.) barber

líhūn 离婚 (v.) divorce

líkāi 离开 (v.) leave, depart

lìkè 立刻 (adv.) immediately

lìliàng 力量 (n.) strength

límǐ 厘米 (n.) centimeter

lǐngdài 领带 (n.) tie

lǐngdǎo 领导 (v., n.) lead; leader

lǐngshì 领事 (n.) consul

lǐngshìguǎn 领事馆 (n.) consulate

lìngyī 另一 (adj.) another, the other

línyīn dàdào 林荫大道 (n.) boulevard

línyù 淋浴 (v.) bathe, take a bath

lìrú 例如 (id.) for example

lìrùn 利润 (n.) profit

lìshǐ 历史 (n.) history

liúlìde 流利的 (adj.) fluent

liúlìde 流利地 (adv.) fluently

liúxíngde 流行的 (adj.) popular

liúxué 留学 (v.) study abroad

liúxuéshēng 留学生 (n.) international /foreign
    student

liúyán 留言 (n., v.) message; leave a message

liùyuè 六月 (n.) June

lǐwù 礼物 (n.) present, gift

lìxiǎn 历险 (n.) adventure

lìyì 利益 (n.) interest

lǐyóu 理由 (n.) reason

lǐyǔ 俚语 (n.) slang

lóngzi 笼子 (n.) cage

lóu 楼 (n.) building, floor (in a hotel, etc.)

lóutī 楼梯 (n.) stair(s)

lù 路 (n.) road

lùqǔ 录取 (v.) admit

luàndiū 乱丢 (v.) litter

lùdì 陆地 (n.) land

lǚfèi 旅费 (n.) fare (air, train, etc.)

lǚguǎn 旅馆 (n.) hotel

lǚguǎn fúwùyuán 旅馆服务员 (n.) bellboy, bellhop

luò xià 落下 (v.) fall (of things)

lǜsède 绿色的 (adj.) green

lǜshī 律师 (n.) attorney, lawyer

lǚxíng 旅行 (v., n.) travel

lǚxíng zhīpiào 旅行支票 (n.) traveler's check(s)

lùyīnjī 录音机 (n.) tape recorder

M

máfan 麻烦 (n.) trouble

mǎi 买 (v.) buy

māma 妈妈 (n.) mother

mànde 慢的 (adj.) slow

mǎnde 满的 (adj.) full

máng 忙 (adj.) busy

mànpǎo 慢跑 (v.) jog

mǎnyìde 满意的 (adj.) satisfied

māo 猫 (n.) cat

màoyì 贸易 (n.) trade

màozi 帽子 (n.) hat

mǎshàng 马上 (adv.) right away

mǎxìtuán 马戏团 (n.) circus

mázuì 麻醉 (n.) anesthesia

měi 美 (n.) beauty

měi 每 (pron.) every

měi tiān 每天 (adv.) everyday

méiguì 玫瑰 (n.) rose

Měiguó 美国 (n.) America

Měiguóde 美国的 (adj.) American

Měiguórén 美国人 (n.) American

Měizhōu 美洲 (n.) America

měilìde 美丽的 (adj.) beautiful

mèimei 妹妹 (n.) younger sister

rìchángde 日常的 (adj.) daily

měiyuán 美元 (n.) dollar

mén 门 (n.) door, gate

ménpiào 门票 (n.) admission ticket

mǐ 米 (n.) rice (raw)

miànbāo 面包 (n.) bread

miànbāochē 面包车 (n.) van

miànbāodiàn 面包店 (n.) bakery

miànbāoshī 面包师 (n.) baker

miǎnfèide 免费的 (adj.) free (free of charge)

miánhua 棉花 (n.) cotton

miànjiá 面颊 (n.) cheek

miǎnshuìde 免税的 (adj.) duty-free

miàntán 面谈 (n.) interview

miǎntiǎnde 腼腆的 (adj.) shy

miào 庙 (n.) temple

miǎoshì 藐视 (n.) contempt

mǐfàn 米饭 (n.) rice (cooked)

mìfēng 蜜蜂 (n.) bee

mǐgāo 米糕 (n.) rice cake

mǐjiǔ 米酒 (n.) rice wine

mílù 迷路 (id.) lose one's way

míngē 民歌 (n.) folk song

míngliàngde 明亮的 (adj.) bright

mìnglìng 命令 (v.) order (sb. to do sth.)

míngtiān 明天 (n.) tomorrow

míngxìnpiàn 明信片 (n.) postcard

míngzhìde 明智的 (adj.) wise

míngzi 名字 (n.) name

mìshū 秘书 (n.) secretary

mìyuè 蜜月 (n.) honeymoon

móhude 模糊的 (adj.) ambiguous

mótuōchē 摩托车 (n.) motorbike, motorcycle

mùbǎn 木板 (n.) board

mùchái 木柴 (n.) firewood

mùdì 墓地 (n.) cemetery

mùlù 目录 (n.) catalog, contents

mùqiánde 目前的 (adj.) current, present

mǔqīn 母亲 (n.) mother

mùshī 牧师 (n.) priest

Mùsīlín 穆斯林 (n.) Muslim

N

ná 拿 (v.) take, hold

nà 那 (pron.) that

nǎilào 奶酪 (n.) cheese

nǎiyóu 奶油 (n.) butter

nánde 男的 (adj.) male

nánfāng 南方 (n.) south

nánfāngde 南方的 (adj.) southern

nánfāngrén 南方人 (n.) southerner

nànmín 难民 (n.) refugee

nánpéngyǒu 男朋友 (n.) boyfriend

nánrén 男人 (n.) man

nánwéiqíngde 难为情的 (adj.) embarrassed

nàozhōng 闹钟 (n.) alarm clock

nèiróng 内容 (n.) content

nèiyī 内衣 (n.) underclothes

néng 能 (aux.) can

nénglì 能力 (n.) ability

nǐ 你 (pron.) you

nián 年 (n.) year

niánde 粘的 (adj.) sticky

niánjí 年级 (n.) grade

niánlíng 年龄 (n.) age

niánqīngde 年轻的 (adj.) young

niǎo 鸟 (n.) bird

nǐde 你的 (pron.) your

níngméngzhī 柠檬汁 (n.) lemonade

ní'nìngde 泥泞的 (adj.) muddy

niú 牛 (n.) cow

niǔkòu 纽扣 (n.) button

niúnǎi 牛奶 (n.) milk

niúròu 牛肉 (n.) beef

nóngchǎng 农场 (n.) farm

nóngcūn 农村 (n.) countryside

nóngmín 农民 (n.) peasant

nüèdài 虐待 (n., v.) abuse

nǚ'ér 女儿 (n.) daughter

nǔhái 女孩 (n.) girl

nǔlì 努力 (adv.) hard, diligently

nǔpéngyou 女朋友 (n.) girlfriend

nǔrén 女人 (n.) woman

nǔshì chènshān 女式衬衫 (n.) blouse

nǔxiūdàoyuàn 女修道院 (n.) convent

nǔxù 女婿 (n.) son-in-law

nǔyǎnyuán 女演员 (n.) actress

O

ǒu'ěr 偶尔 (adv.) occasionally

P

pá 爬 (v.) climb, crawl

pái 排 (n.) row (of seats)

pāimài 拍卖 (n.) auction

pāizhào 拍照 (v.) take a picture

pàngde 胖的 (adj.) fat

pángguāng 膀胱 (n.) bladder

pángxiè 螃蟹 (n.) crab

pánzi 盘子 (n.) dish, plate

pǎo 跑 (v.) run

páshǒu 扒手 (n.) pickpocket

péitóng 陪同 (v.) accompany, escort

pén 盆 (n.) basin

pēngtiáo 烹调 (v.) cook

péngyou 朋友 (n.) friend

pèngzhuàng 碰撞 (v., n.) collide; collision

piān'ài 偏爱 (v.) prefer

piányide 便宜的 (adj.) cheap, inexpensive

piào 票 (n.) ticket

piǎobái 漂白 (v.) bleach

piàoliangde 漂亮的 (adj.) pretty

pīfā 批发 (n.) wholesale

píjiǔ 啤酒 (n.) beer

píjuànde 疲倦的 (adj.) tired

píngchángde 平常的 (adj.) ordinary

píngděngde 平等的 (adj.) equal

pínghéng 平衡 (n.) balance

píngjūn 平均 (n.) average

pínglùn 评论 (n.) comment

píngguǒ 苹果 (n.) apple

píngzi 瓶子 (n.) bottle

pínkùn 贫困 (n.) poverty

pīnxiě 拼写 (v.) spell

pínxuě 贫血 (n.) anemia

pīpíng 批评 (n., v.) criticism; criticize

pīzhǔn 批准 (v.) approve

pùbù 瀑布 (n.) waterfall

pǔtōngde 普通的 (adj.) common, ordinary

Q

qí 骑 (v.) ride (a bike)

qī 期 (n.) issue (magazine)

qī 漆 (n.) lacquer

qián 钱 (n.) money

qiàn 欠 (v.) owe

qiān 千 (n.) thousand

qiánbāo 钱包 (n.) purse, wallet

lěngpán 冷盘 (n.) appetizer, cold dish

qiángdàde 强大的 (adj.) powerful, strong

qiǎngjié 抢劫 (v.) rob

qiānmíng 签名 (v., n.) sign; signature

qiǎnzé 谴责 (v., n.) condemn, condemnation

qiānzhèng 签证 (n.) visa

qiáo 桥 (n.) bridge

qiāo 敲 (v.) knock

qǐchuáng 起床 (v.) get up

qiē 切 (v.) cut

qǐfēi 起飞 (v.) take off (plane)

qìfèn 气愤 (adj.) angry

qǐgài 乞丐 (n.) beggar

qìhòu 气候 (n.) climate

qímiàode 奇妙的 (adj.) wonderful

qǐng 请 (v.) please (polite)

qīngchǔde 清楚的 (adj.) clear

qīngchǔde 清楚地 (adv.) clearly

qīngchūnqī 青春期 (n.) adolescence

qīngde 轻的 (adj.) light

qīngjiéde 清洁的 (adj.) clean

qǐngkè 请客 (v.) treat (sb. to meal)

qíngkuàng 情况 (n.) condition, situation

qínglǎngde 晴朗的 (adj.) sunny

qìngzhù 庆祝 (v., n.) celebrate, celebration

qīnjìnde 亲近的 (adj.) close (near in friendship)

qǐnjù 寝具 (n.) bedding

qīnlüè 侵略 (n.) aggression

qínmiǎnde 勤勉的 (adj.) diligent

qīnqì 亲戚 (n.) relative(s)

qióngde 穷的 (adj.) poor

qīpiàn 欺骗 (v.) cheat

qǐqiú 乞求 (v.) beg

qiú 球 (n.) ball

qiūtiān 秋天 (n.) fall (autumn)

qìyóu 汽油 (n.) gas, petrol

qīyuè 七月 (n.) July

qīzi 妻子 (n.) wife

qù 去 (v.) go

qū 区 (n.) district

quàngào 劝告 (v.) advise

quánjī 拳击 (n.) boxing

quánwēi 权威 (n.) authority

quányù 痊愈 (v.) recover (from illness)

quánzhíde 全职的 (adj.) full-time

qǔbǎojīn 取保金 (n.) bail

qǔdé 取得 (v.) achieve

quèqiède 确切地 (adv.) definitely

quèrèn 确认 (v.) confirm

quēxí 缺席 (n.) absence

qūxiàn 曲线 (n.) curve

qǔxiāo 取消 (v., n.) cancel; cancellation

R

ràng 让 (v.) let

ránhòu 然后 (adv.) then

rèdài 热带 (n.) tropics

rède 热的 (adj.) hot

rén 人 (n.) person

réngrán 仍然 (adv.) still

rènhé 任何 (adj.) any

rènhérén 任何人 (pron.) anybody

rénkǒu 人口 (n.) population

rénqún 人群 (n.) crowd

rěnshòu 忍受 (v.) bear

rénwù 人物 (n.) character(s)

rénxíngdào 人行道 (n.) crossing

rénzàode 人造的 (adj.) artificial

rènwéi 认为 (v.) think

rènzhēnde 认真的 (adj.) serious, conscientious

rìchū 日出 (n.) sunrise

rìlì 日历 (n.) calendar

rìluò 日落 (n.) sunset

róngqì 容器 (n.) container

róngyìde 容易的 (adj.) easy

ròu 肉 (n.) meat

ruǎnde 软的 (adj.) soft

rùchǎngquàn 入场券 (n.) admission ticket

rǔfáng 乳房 (n.) breast

rúguǒ 如果 (conj.) if

rùkǒu 入口 (n.) entrance

ruòde 弱的 (adj.) weak

S

sǎn 伞 (n.) umbrella

sànbù 散步 (v.) take a walk

sānyuè 三月 (n.) March

sàozhou 扫帚 (n.) broom

sēnlín 森林 (n.) forest

shāfā 沙发 (n.) couch

shālā 沙拉 (n.) salad

shān 山 (n.) mountain

shāndòng 山洞 (n.) cave

shàng 上 (adv.) up

shàng chē 上车 (v.) get on (a bus)

shàng ge yuè 上个月 (n.) last month

shàngbān 上班 (v.) go to work

shāngcánde 伤残的 (adj.) disabled

shàngchuáng 上床 (v.) go to bed

shāngdiàn 商店 (n.) store

shāngrén 商人 (n.) businessperson

shāngǔ 山谷 (n.) valley

shàngwǔ 上午 (n.) morning

shàngxué 上学 (v.) go to school

shāngyè 商业 (n.) business, commerce

shēngyì 生意 (n.) business

shàngyī 上衣 (n.) jacket

shāo 烧 (v.) burn

shǎode 少的 (adj.) little, few

shāokǎo 烧烤 (v.) grill

shǎoshù 少数 (n.) minority

shǎoshù mínzú 少数民族 (n.) ethnic minority

shèhuì 社会 (n.) society

shèhuì gōngzuòzhě 社会工作者 (n.) social
    worker

shèjiāo jùhuì 社交聚会 (n.) party

shěng 省 (n.) province

shèng 胜 (v.) win

shēngchǎn 生产 (v., n.) produce; production

Shèngdànjié 圣诞节 (n.) Christmas

shēngde 生的 (adj.) raw

shēnghuó fāngshì 生活方式 (n.) lifestyle

shēnghuó shuǐpíng 生活水平 (n.) standard of living

Shèngjīng 圣经 (n.) Bible

shēnghuó 生活 (n.) life

shēngrì 生日 (n.) birthday

shéngzi 绳子 (n.) rope

shēngyīn 声音 (n.) sound, voice

shénme 什么 (pron.) what

shénme shíhou 什么时候 (ques.) when

shēnqǐng 申请 (v., n.) apply, application

shēntǐ 身体 (n.) body, health

shí 十 (n.) ten

shì 是 (v.) be

shì 试 (v.) try

shī 诗 (n.) poem

shì 事 (n.) thing (matter)

shìbīng 士兵 (n.) soldier

shìchǎng 市场 (n.) market

shìdàngde 适当的 (adj.) appropriate

shí'èryuè 十二月 (n.) December

shìgù 事故 (n.) accident

shìhé 适合 (v.) fit

shìjì 世纪 (n.) century

shíjiān 时间 (n.) time

shìjiè 世界 (n.) world

shíjìshang 实际上 (adv.) actually

shíkè 时刻 (n.) moment

shīmíng 失明 (n.) blindness

shītǐ 尸体 (n.) corpse

shīwàngde 失望的 (adj.) disappointed

shíwù 食物 (n.) food

shīyède 失业的 (adj.) unemployed

shíyì 十亿 (n.) billion

shíyīyuè 十一月 (n.) November

shǐyòng 使用 (v.) use

shíyòngde 实用的 (adj.) practical

shíyù 食欲 (n.) appetite

shíyuè 十月 (n.) October

shízìlùkǒu 十字路口 (n.) intersection

shǒu 手 (n.) hand

shǒubì 手臂 (n.) arm

shǒubiǎo 手表 (n.) wristwatch

shōudào 收到 (v.) receive (sth.)

shòude 瘦的 (adj.) thin (describing people)

shǒudiàntǒng 手电筒 (n.) flashlight

shǒudū 首都 (n.) capital (city)

shǒugōng zhìzuòde 手工制作的 (adj.) handmade

shǒugōngyì 手工艺 (n.) handicraft

shōuhuò 收获 (n.) harvest

shǒujī 手机 (n.) cell phone

shōují 收集 (v.) collect

shōujù 收据 (n.) receipt

shōukuǎnyuán 收款员 (n.) cashier

shòuquán 授权 (v., n.) authorize; authorization

shōurù 收入 (n.) income

shǒushù 手术 (n.) surgery

shǒutíxiāng 手提箱 (n.) suitcase

shōuyǎng 收养 (v.) adopt (a child)

shōuyīnjī 收音机 (n.) radio

shǒuzhàng 手杖 (n.) cane

shǒuzhuó 手镯 (n.) bracelet

shù 束 (n.) bunch

shù 树 (n.) tree

shǔ 数 (v.) count

shū 书 (n.) book

shuāzi 刷子 (n.) brush

shuāngyǔde 双语的 (adj.) bilingual

shūcài 蔬菜 (n.) vegetable(s)

shūdiàn 书店 (n.) bookstore

shuí 谁 (pron.) who

shuì 睡 (v.) sleep

shuì 税 (n.) tax

shuǐ 水 (n.) water

shuìdài 睡袋 (n.) sleeping bag

shuǐguǒ 水果 (n.) fruit

shuǐniú 水牛 (n.) water buffalo

shuǐpào 水泡 (n.) blister

shuǐzāi 水灾 (n.) flood

shūjià 书架 (n.) bookcase

shùkǒu 漱口 (v.) rinse (one's mouth)

shúliànde 熟练的 (adj.) skilled

shùliàng 数量 (n.) amount, quantity

shùlín 树林 (n.) woods (forest)

shuō 说 (v.) say, speak

shuōmíng 说明 (v., n.) indicate; indication

shúrén 熟人 (n.) acquaintance

shūshìde 舒适的 (adj.) comfortable

shūshu 叔叔 (n.) uncle

shúshuìde 熟睡的 (adj.) asleep

shùyè 树叶 (n.) leaf

shǔyú 属于 (v.) belong to

shùzì 数字 (n.) number

shūzi 梳子 (n.) comb

sǐ 死 (v., n.) die; death

sīchóu 丝绸 (n.) silk

sī'niàn 思念 (v.) miss

sīrénde 私人的 (adj.) private

sìyuè 四月 (n.) April

sòng (huò) 送 (货) (v.) deliver

suàn le 算了 (id.) never mind

suānde 酸的 (adj.) sour

sūdá 苏打 (n.) soda

sūdǎshuǐ 苏打水 (n.) soda water

sùdù jíxiàn 速度极限 (n.) speed limit

suíbiànde 随便的 (adj.) casual

suīrán 虽然 (conj.) although

suìxiè 碎屑 (n.) crumb

sūnzi 孙子 (n.) grandson

sūnnǚ 孙女 (n.) granddaughter

suōduǎn 缩短 (v.) shorten

suōxiě 缩写 (n.) abbreviation

suǒyǐ 所以 (adv.) therefore

suǒyǒude 所有的 (adj.) all

suǒ 锁 (n., v.) lock

sùshè 宿舍 (n.) dormitory

T

tā 他 (pron.) he

tā 她 (pron.) she

tāde 他的 (pron.) his

tài duō 太多 (exp.) too much/many

tàidu 态度 (n.) attitude

tàitai 太太 (n.) Mrs., wife

tàiyang 太阳 (n.) sun

tàiyangjing 太阳镜 (n.) sunglasses

tāmen 他们 (pron.) they

tāmende 他们的 (pron.) their

tán 谈 (v.) talk

tǎnbái 坦白 (v., n.) confess; confession

táng 糖 (n.) sugar

tāng 汤 (n.) soup

tǎng 躺 (v.) lie down

tāngchí 汤匙 (n.) spoon

tángguǒ 糖果 (n.) candy

tāngmiàn 汤面 (n.) noodle soup

tǎnzi 毯子 (n.) blanket

tǎojià huánjià 讨价还价 (v.) bargain

tǎolùn 讨论 (n., v.) discusion; discuss

táoqì 陶器 (n.) pottery

tèbiéde 特别的 (adj.) special

téngtòng 疼痛 (n.) ache, pain

téngtòngde 疼痛的 (adj.) painful (sore)

tián 田 (n.) field (paddy)

tiān 天 (n.) day, sky

tiánde 甜的 (adj.) sweet

tiānhuābǎn 天花板 (n.) ceiling

tiānkōng 天空 (n.) sky

tiānqì 天气 (n.) weather

tiānshǐ 天使 (n.) angel

tiānxiàn 天线 (n.) antenna

Tiānzhǔjiàotú 天主教徒 (n.) Catholic

tiáojiàn 条件 (n.) condition, term

tiàowǔ 跳舞 (n., v.) dance

tiáozhěng 调整 (v.) adjust

tígòng 提供 (v.) provide

tíng 停 (v.) stop, park

tīng 听 (v.) listen

tíngchēchǎng 停车场 (n.) parking lot

tīng dào 听到 (v.) hear

tǐyùchǎng 体育场 (n.) stadium

tǒng 桶 (n.) bucket

tōngguò 通过 (v.) pass

tóngnián 童年 (n.) childhood

tóngshì 同事 (n.) colleague

tōngxìn 通信 (n.) correspondence

tōngxùn 通讯 (n.) communications

tóngyì 同意 (v.) agree

tōngzhī 通知 (n.) announcement

tóu 头 (n.) head

tōu 偷 (v.) steal

tóufa 头发 (n.) hair

tóupiào 投票 (v.) vote

tóutòng 头痛 (n.) headache

tóuzī 投资 (n., v.) investment; invest

tuán 团 (n.) group

tūde 秃的 (adj.) bald

tǔdì 土地 (n.) land

túfū 屠夫 (n.) butcher

tuī 推 (v.) push

tuījiàn 推荐 (v., n.) recommend,
　　recommendation

tuìxiū 退休 (v.) retire (from working)

tújìng 途径 (n.) approach

tuō diào 脱掉 (v.) take off (clothes)

tuōpán 托盘 (n.) tray

tuōxié 拖鞋 (n.) slipper(s)

tūrán 突然 (adv.) suddenly

túshūguǎn 图书馆 (n.) library

T-xùshān T恤衫 (n.) T-shirt

W

wàiguó 外国的 (adj.) foreign

wàiguórén 外国人 (n.) foreigner

wàijiāoguān 外交官 (n.) diplomat

wàimian 外面 (adv.) outside

wàiqiáo 外侨 (n.) alien

wàisūn 外孙 (n.) grandson

wàisūnnǚ 外孙女 (n.) granddaughter

wán 玩 (v.) play

wǎn 碗 (n.) bowl

wǎncān 晚餐 (n.) dinner

wánchéng 完成 (n.) completion

wǎnchú 碗橱 (n.) cupboard

wǎnde 晚的 (adj.) late

wàngjì 忘记 (v.) forget

wǎngqiú 网球 (n.) tennis

wǎnshang 晚上 (n.) evening

wánzhěngde 完整的 (adj., v.) complete

wèi 喂 (v.) feed

wèidao 味道 (n.) taste

wéidōu 围兜 (n.) bib

wēifēng 微风 (n.) breeze

wéijīn 围巾 (n.) scarf

wèilái 未来 (n.) future

wèile 为了 (prep.) for the sake of, in order to

wèishēngzhǐ 卫生纸 (n.) toilet paper

wèishénme 为什么 (adv.) why

wēixiǎnde 危险的 (adj.) dangerous

wēixiào 微笑 (n., v.) smile

wěiyuánhuì 委员会 (n.) committee

wén 闻 (v.) smell

wèn 问 (v.) ask

wēndù 温度 (n.) temperature

wénhuà 文化 (n.) culture

wénmíng 文明 (n.) civilization

wēnnuǎnde 温暖的 (adj.) warm

wèntí 问题 (n.) question

wénxué 文学 (n.) literature

wénzhāng 文章 (n.) article

wénzi 蚊子 (n.) mosquito

wǒ 我 (pron.) I

wǒde 我的 (pron.) my

wǒmen 我们 (pron.) we

wǒmende 我们的 (pron.) our

wòshì 卧室 (n.) bedroom

wǔfàn 午饭 (n.) lunch

wùhuì 误会 (n.) misunderstanding

wǔdǎo 舞蹈 (n.) dance

wǔhuì 舞会 (n.) ball (dancing)

wūrǎn 污染 (n., v.) pollution; contaminate

wǔtīng 舞厅 (n.) ballroom

wǔyè 午夜 (n.) midnight

wǔyuè 五月 (n.) May

X

xī 西 (n.) west

xǐ 洗 (v.) wash

xì 系 (n.) department (at a college)

xīzhuāng 西装 (n.) suit

xià 下 (adv.) down

xiā 虾 (n.) shrimp

xià chē 下车 (v.) get off (a bus)

xià'è 下颚 (n.) chin

xiāde 瞎的 (adj.) blind

xiàn 线 (n.) thread, string, line

xiàndàide 现代的 (adj.) modern

xiánde 咸的 (adj.) salty

xiǎnde 显得 (v.) look (appear)

xiàng 象 (v., prep.) resemble; like

xiāngcūn 乡村 (n.) countryside

xiàng 向 (prep.) to, toward

xiǎng 想 (v.) think

xiāngbīnjiǔ 香槟酒 (n.) champagne

xiǎngfǎ 想法 (n.) idea, thought

xiàngliàn 项链 (n.) necklace

xiǎngshòu 享受 (n., v.) enjoyment; enjoy

xiāngsìde 相似的 (adj.) alike

xiāngtóngde 相同的 (adj.) same

xiāngxìn 相信 (v.) believe

xiāngyān 香烟 (n.) cigarette

xiànjīn 现金 (n.) cash

xiānsheng 先生 (n.) Mr., husband

xiànzài 现在 (adv.) now

xiào 笑 (v.) laugh

xiǎode 小的 (adj.) small, little

xiǎofèi 小费 (n.) tip (gratuity)

Xiǎojie 小姐 (n.) Miss

xiǎoshí 小时 (n.) hour

xiǎoshuō 小说 (n.) novel

xiǎotōu 小偷 (n.) burglar, thief

xiǎoxīn 小心 (v.) beware

xiǎoxīnde 小心的 (adj.) careful, cautious

xiǎoxué 小学 (n.) elementary school

xiàtiān 夏天 (n.) summer

xiàwǔ 下午 (n.) afternoon

xiázhǎide 狭窄的 (adj.) narrow

xìbāo 细胞 (n.) cell

xiě 写 (v.) write

xiédài 携带 (v.) carry

xiéhuì 协会 (n.) association

xièhuò 卸货 (v.) unload

xièxie 谢谢 (v.) thank you

xiéyì 协议 (n.) agreement

xiézhù 协助 (v.) assist

xiézi 鞋子 (n.) shoe

xiězuò 写作 (v.) compose

xīfāng 西方 (n.) the West

xīfāngde 西方的 (adj.) western

xīfāngrén 西方人 (n.) Westerner

xǐfàyè 洗发液 (n.) shampoo

xífù 媳妇 (n.) daughter-in-law

xíguàn 习惯 (n., v.) habit; be used to

xīhóngshì 西红柿 (n.) tomato

xǐhuan 喜欢 (v.) like

xìjūn 细菌 (n.) bacteria

xímèngsī 席梦思 (n.) mattress

xìn 信 (n.) letter (to a friend)

xīnde 新的 (adj.) new

xìnfēng 信封 (n.) envelope

xìng 姓 (n.) surname

xīng 星 (n.) star

xíngdòng 行动 (n.) action

xìngfú 幸福 (n.) happiness

xǐng lái 醒来 (v.) wake up

xíngli 行李 (n.) baggage, luggage

xīngqī 星期 (n.) week

xíngróngcí 形容词 (n.) adjective

xíngwéi 行为 (n.) behavior, conduct

xìngyùnde 幸运的 (adj.) lucky

xīnláng 新郎 (n.) groom

xìnniàn 信念 (n.) belief

xīnniáng 新娘 (n.) bride

xìnrèn 信任 (n., v.) trust

xīnwén 新闻 (n.) news

xìnxī 信息 (n.) information

xīnxiānde 新鲜的 (adj.) fresh

xìnxīn 信心 (n.) confidence

xìnyòngkǎ 信用卡 (n.) credit card

xióng 熊 (n.) bear

xiōng 胸 (n.) chest

xiōngzhào 胸罩 (n.) bra

xǐqìngde 喜庆的 (adj.) festive

xīshōu 吸收 (v.) absorb

xísú 习俗 (n.) custom

xiùkǒu 袖口 (n.) cuff

xiūlǐ 修理 (v.) repair

xiūxi 休息 (n., v.) rest

xiùzi 袖子 (n.) sleeve

xīwàng 希望 (n., v.) hope

xǐyīfáng 洗衣房 (n.) laundry room

xīyǐn 吸引 (v.) attract

xīyǐnrénde 吸引人的 (adj.) attractive

xǐzǎo 洗澡 (v.) take a bath/shower

xízi 席子 (n.) mat (sleeping mat)

xuányá 悬崖 (n.) cliff

xuányūn 眩晕 (adj.) dizzy

xuǎnzé 选择 (n., v.) choice; choose

xǔduō 许多 (adj.) much, many

xuē 削 (v.) peel

xuě 雪 (n.) snow

xuéfèi 学费 (n.) tuition

xuějiā 雪茄 (n.) cigar

xuénián 学年 (n.) academic year

xuéqī 学期 (n.) academic term

xuésheng 学生 (n.) student

xuéshùde 学术的 (adj.) academic

xuétú 学徒 (n.) apprentice

xuéwèi 学位 (n.) degree (diploma)

xuéxí 学习 (n., v.) study

xuéxiào 学校 (n.) school

xuéyuàn 学院 (n.) college

xuēzi 靴子 (n.) boot

xǔkězhèng 许可证 (n.) permit

xùnliàn 训练 (v.) train

xùnsùde 迅速地 (adv.) quickly

xūyào 需要 (n., v.) need

Y

yáchǐ 牙齿 (n.) tooth

yán 盐 (n.) salt

yǎngjiā 养家 (v.) support (one's family)

yājīn 押金 (n.) deposit

yàngpǐn 样品 (n.) sample

yángtái 阳台 (n.) balcony

yànhuì 宴会 (n.) banquet

yān 烟 (n.) smoke, cigarette

yānhuīgāng 烟灰缸 (n.) ashtray

yǎnjing 眼睛 (n.) eye

yǎnjìng 眼镜 (n.) eyeglasses

yánjiū 研究 (n., v.) research

yánjiūyuán 研究员 (n.) researcher

yǎnmái 掩埋 (v.) bury

yánsè 颜色 (n.) color

yànyǔ 谚语 (n.) proverb

yǎnyuán 演员 (n.) actor

yào 药 (n.) drug (medicine)

yào 要 (v.) want

yǎo 咬 (v.) bite

yāo 腰 (n.) waist

yáolán 摇篮 (n.) cradle

yāoqǐng 邀请 (n., v.) invitation; invite

yàoshi 钥匙 (n.) key

yàowán 药丸 (n.) pill

yáyī 牙医 (n.) dentist

Yàzhōu 亚洲 (n.) Asia

Yàzhōude 亚洲的 (adj.) Asian

Yàzhōurén 亚洲人 (n.) Asian

yè 页 (n.) page

yě 也 (adv.) also

yèlǐ 夜里 (n.) night

yèwō 腋窝 (n.) armpit

yěxǔ 也许 (adv.) perhaps

yī 一 (n.) one

yídìng 一定 (adv.) surely, certainly

yìbān 一般 (adj., adv.) general, usual; usually

yìděng 一等 (adj.) first-class

yīfu 衣服 (n.) clothes

yǐhūnde 已婚的 (adj.) married

yìjiàn 意见 (n.) opinion, comment

yǐjing 已经 (adv.) already

yīliáo 医疗 (n.) health (medical care)

yīmàojiān 衣帽间 (n.) checkroom

yín 银 (n.) silver

yíng 赢 (v.) win

yìngbì 硬币 (n.) coin

yìngde 硬的 (adj.) hard (of objects)

yīng'ér 婴儿 (n.) baby

yīnggāi 应该 (aux.) ought to; should

yīngjùnde 英俊的 (adj.) handsome

yīngwén 英文 (n.) English (language)

yǐngxiǎng 影响 (n., v.) influence

yìngzhǐbǎn 硬纸板 (n.) cardboard

yínháng 银行 (n.) bank

yínhángjiā 银行家 (n.) banker

yǐnliào 饮料 (n.) beverage

yǐnqǐ 引起 (v.) cause

yìnshuā 印刷 (v.) print

yīnwèi 因为 (conj.) because

yǐnxíng yǎnjìng 隐形眼镜 (n.) contact lenses

Yīngyǔ 英语 (n.) English (language)

yīnyuè 音乐 (n.) music

yīnyuèhuì 音乐会 (n.) concert

yīnyuèjiā 音乐家 (n.) musician

yìqǐ 一起 (adv.) together

yǐqián 以前 (adv.) ago, before (when telling time)

yíqiè 一切 (pron.) everything

yīshēng 医生 (n.) doctor

yìshù 艺术 (n.) art

yìshùjiā 艺术家 (n.) artist

yìsībùgǒude 一丝不苟的 (adj.) meticulous

yīyuàn 医院 (n.) hospital

yīyuè 一月 (n.) January

yìzhí 一直 (adv.) straight

yǐzi 椅子 (n.) chair

yōngbào 拥抱 (v.) hug

yōngjǐde 拥挤的 (adj.) crowded

yòngjīn 佣金 (n.) commission

yòngjù 用具 (n.) appliance

yōngyǒu 拥有 (v.) own

yóu 油 (n.) oil

yǒu 有 (v.) have

yòubian 右边 (n.) right (turn right)

yǒubìngde 有病的 (adj.) ill, sick

yòu'ěr 诱饵 (n.) bait

yǒufēngde 有风的 (adj.) windy

yǒuhǎode 友好的 (adj.) friendly

yóujiàn 邮件 (n.) mail

yǒujiàzhíde 有价值的 (adj.) valuable

yóujú 邮局 (n.) post office

yóukè 游客 (n.) tourist

yǒulìde 有利的 (adj.) advantageous

yǒulǐde 有礼地 (adj.) courteous

yǒulǐmàode 有礼貌的 (adj.) polite

yōulǜ 忧虑 (n.) concern, anxiety

yǒumíngde 有名的 (adj.) famous

yǒunénglìde 有能力的 (adj.) able, capable

yóupiào 邮票 (n.) stamp

yǒuqiánde 有钱的 (adj.) rich (wealthy)

yǒuqùde 有趣的 (adj.) interesting

yǒushí 有时 (adv.) sometimes

yōushì 优势 (n.) advantage

yǒuxiàn diànshì 有线电视 (n.) cable TV

yǒuyì 友谊 (n.) friendship

yǒuyìshíde 有意识的 (adj.) conscious, deliberate

yóuyǒng 游泳 (v.) swim

yóuyǒngchí 游泳池 (n.) swimming pool

yǒuyòngde 有用的 (adj.) useful

yóuyǒngyī 游泳衣 (n.) bathing suit

yóuyú 由于 (id.) thanks to, due to

yóuzhà 油炸 (v.) fry

yú 鱼 (n.) fish

yúkuàide 愉快的 (adj.) enjoyable, pleasant

yùfùkuǎn 预付款 (n.) advance (money)

yǔ 雨 (n.) rain

yuǎn 远 (adj.) far

yuángōng 员工 (n.) staff

yuánquān 圆圈 (n.) circle

yuánzhù 援助 (n.) aid

yuánzhūbǐ 圆珠笔 (n.) ballpoint pen

yuànzi 院子 (n.) courtyard

yuǎnzú 远足 (v.) hike

yùdìng 预订 (v.) reserve

yuè 月 (n.) month

yuē shíjiān 约时间 (id.) schedule an appointment

yuèduì 乐队 (n.) band

yuēhuì 约会 (n.) appointment

yuèliang 月亮 (n.) moon

yuèqì 乐器 (n.) musical instrument

yuètái 月台 (n.) platform (railway)

yùgāng 浴缸 (n.) bathtub

yùjiàn 遇见 (v.) run into sb.

yúkuàide 愉快的 (adj.) cheerful, pleasant

yúmín 渔民 (n.) fisherman

yún 云 (n.) cloud

yùndòng 运动 (n.) sport

yùndòngyuán 运动员 (n.) athlete

yǔnnuò 允诺 (n., v.) promise

yǔnxǔ 允许 (n., v.) permission; permit, allow

yùsuàn 预算 (n.) budget

yǔyán 语言 (n.) language

yùyī 浴衣 (n.) bathrobe

yǔyī 雨衣 (n.) raincoat

Z

zài 再 (adv.) again

zài 在 (prep.) at

zài hòumian 在后面 (adv.) back

zài lǐmiàn 在里面 (adv.) inside

zài lóushàng 在楼上 (adv.) upstairs

zài lóuxià 在楼下 (adv.) downstairs

zài nàli 在那里 (adv.) there

zài nǎr 在哪儿 (adv.) where

zài pángbiān 在旁边 (adv.) aside

zài qiánmian 在前面 (adv.) ahead

zài...duìmiàn 在…对面 (id.) across from, opposite

zài...lǐ 在…里 (id.) in

zài...pángbiān 在…旁边 (id.) beside, next to

zài...qījiān 在…期间 (id.) during

zài...shàng 在…上 (id.) on, over, above

zài...xià 在…下 (id.) below, under

zài...hòu 在…后 (id.) after, behind

zài...wàimian 在…外面(prep.) outside

zài...zhījiān 在…之间 (id.) between

zài...qián 在…前 (id.) before, in front of

zài...zhōng 在…中 (id.) among

zàijiàn! 再见! (exp.) bye-bye!

zāi'nàn 灾难 (n.) disaster

zànchéng 赞成 (v.) approve

zāngde 脏的 (adj.) dirty

zànglǐ 葬礼 (n.) funeral

zànshíde 暂时的 (adj.) temporary

zǎo 早 (adj., adv.) early

zǎocān 早餐 (n.) breakfast

zǎoshang 早上 (n.) morning

záwù 杂务 (n.) chore

zázhì 杂志 (n.) magazine

zēngjiā 增加 (n., v.) increase

zérèn 责任 (n.) responsibility

zhàdàn 炸弹 (n.) bomb

zhàn 站 (v., n.) stand; station

zhāng 章 (n.) chapter

zhǎng dà 长大 (v.) grow up

zhàngdān 帐单 (n.) check (at a restaurant)

zhàngfu 丈夫 (n.) husband

zhànghù 账户 (n.) account

zhàngpeng 帐篷 (n.) tent

zhǎnlǎn 展览 (n.) exhibition

zhànzhēng 战争 (n.) war

zhǎo 找 (v.) look for

zhǎo dào 找到 (v.) find

zhàoguǎn háizi 照管孩子 (v.) baby-sit

zhàopiàn 照片 (n.) photograph

zhàoxiàngjī 照像机 (n.) camera

zhǎyǎn 眨眼 (v.) blink

zhè 这 (pron.) this

zhèlǐ 这里 (adv.) here

zhēn 针 (n.) needle

zhēnchéngde 真诚的 (adj.) sincere

zhēnde ma? 真的吗? (exp.) really?

zhèng 挣 (v.) earn (a salary)

zhèngcè 政策 (n.) policy

zhèngchángde 正常的 (adj.) normal

zhěngjiéde 整洁的 (adj.) neat, tidy

zhēnglùn 争论 (v., n.) argue; argument

zhèngquède 正确的 (adj.) right, correct

zhèr 这儿 (adv.) here

zhèngshìde 正式的 (adj.) formal

zhēnshíde 真实的 (adj.) real, authentic

zhěnsuǒ 诊所 (n.) clinic

zhěntou 枕头 (n.) pillow

zhěntóutào 枕头套 (n.) pillowcase

zhèngzhì 政治 (n.) politics

zhǐ 只 (adv.) only

zhǐ 纸 (n.) paper

zhīdào 知道 (v.) know

zhìfú 制服 (n.) uniform

zhǐxiāng 纸箱 (n.) carton

zhǐhuī 指挥 (v.) direct

zhǐkòng 指控 (v., n.) accuse; accusation

zhìliàng 质量 (n.) quality

zhǐ'nánzhēn 指南针 (n.) compass

zhīpiào 支票 (n.) check

zhīpiàoběn 支票本 (n.) checkbook

zhìyù 治愈 (n.) cure

zhìyuànzhě 志愿者 (n.) volunteer

zhìzào 制造 (v.) manufacture, make

zhízhào 执照 (n.) license

zhǒng 种 (n.) kind, type

zhòng 种 (v.) plant (rice)

zhōng 钟 (n.) clock

zhòngde 重的 (adj.) heavy

zhōnggào 忠告 (n.) advice

zhōngcān 中餐 (n.) lunch

Zhōngguó 中国 (n.) China

Zhōngguóde 中国的 (adj.) Chinese

Zhōngguórén 中国人 (n.) Chinese

zhōngjiān 中间 (n.) middle

zhōngjíde 中级的 (adj.) intermediate (level)

zhōngwǔ 中午 (n.) noon

zhōngxīn 中心 (n.) center

zhōngxīnde 中心的 (adj.) central

zhòngyàode 重要的 (adj.) important

zhōu 州 (n.) state (of the fifty states)

zhōumò 周末 (n.) weekend

zhōunián 周年 (n.) anniversary

zhōuwéi 周围 (n.) vicinity, surrounding

Zhōngwén 中文 (n.) Chinese

zhù 住 (v.) live

zhǔyi 主意 (n.) idea

zhǔ 煮 (v.) boil

zhuā 抓 (v.) catch

zhuāngjia 庄稼 (n.) crop

zhuàngkuàng 状况 (n.) circumstance

zhuǎnhuàn 转换 (v.) convert

zhuānlán 专栏 (n.) column (in a newspaper)

zhuǎnwān 转弯 (v.) turn

zhuānxīnde 专心的 (adj.) attentive

zhuǎnzhàng 转帐 (v.) transfer (money)

zhùchù 住处 (n.) accommodations

zhùfú 祝福 (v.) bless

zhǔfù 主妇 (n.) homemaker

zhùhè 祝贺 (v.) congratulate

zhùhè nǐ 祝贺你 (interj.) congratulations

zhǔnquède 准确的 (adj.) accurate

zhǔnshí 准时 (adv., adj.) on time; punctual

zhuólù 着陆 (v.) land

zhuōzi 桌子 (n.) table

zhǔrèn 主任 (n.) director

zhūròu 猪肉 (n.) pork

zhùshǒu 助手 (n.) assistant

zhǔxí 主席 (n.) chairperson

zhǔxiū 主修 (v., n.) major (in)

zhǔyì 主意 (n.) idea

zhùyì 注意 (v.) pay attention

zhúzi 竹子 (n.) bamboo

zì...yǐlái 自…以来 (conj.) since

zīběn 资本 (n.) capital (money)

zǐdàn 子弹 (n.) bullet

zìdiǎn 字典 (n.) dictionary

zìdòngde 自动的 (adj.) automatic

zìjǐde 自己的 (adj.) one's own, self

zìmǔbiǎo 字母表 (n.) alphabet

zìrán 自然 (n.) nature

zìránde 自然的 (adj.) natural

zǐxìde 仔细地 (adv.) carefully

zìxíngchē 自行车 (n.) bicycle

zǒnggòng 总共 (adv.) altogether

zōnghéde 综合的 (adj.) comprehensive

zōngjiào 宗教 (n.) religion

zōngsède 棕色的 (adj.) brown

zǒngshì 总是 (adv.) always

zǒngshù 总数 (n.) total

zǒngtǒng 总统 (n.) president (of a country)

zǒuláng 走廊 (n.) hallway

zū 租 (v.) rent

zǔ 组 (n.) group

zúgòude 足够的 (adj.) enough

zuǐ 嘴 (n.) mouth

zuìhǎode 最好的 (adj.) best

zūjīn 租金 (n.) rent (money)

zūnjìng 尊敬 (n., v.) respect

zūnjìngde 尊敬的 (adj.) honored, respectful

zuò 做 (v.) do

zuò 坐 (v.) sit

zuò fēijī 坐飞机 (v.) fly (take a plane)

zuò guǎnggào 做广告 (v.) advertise

zuǒbian 左边 (n.) left (turn left)

zuòdiàn 坐垫 (n.) cushion

zuòjiā 作家 (n.) author, writer

zuótiān 昨天 (n.) yesterday

zuówǎn 昨晚 (n.) last night

zuòwèi 座位 (n.) seat

zuòwén 作文 (n.) composition

zúqiú 足球 (n.) football (soccer)

zǔxiān 祖先 (n.) ancestor

zǔzhī 组织 (v., n.) organize; organization

zuòbì 作弊 (v.) cheat

ENGLISH-CHINESE DICTIONARY

A

a (art.) 一 yī

a.m. (n.) 上午 shàngwǔ

abandon (v.) 放弃 fàngqì

abbreviation (n.) 缩写 suōxiě

ability (n.) 能力 nénglì

able (adj.) 有能力的 yǒunénglìde

abnormal (adj.) 反常的 fǎnchángde

aboard (adv.) 在船上 zài chuán shàng

abortion (n.) 堕胎 duòtāi

about (prep.) 大约 dàyuē

above (prep.) 在…之上 zài...zhīshàng

abroad (adv.) 国外 guówài

absence (n.) 缺席 quēxí

absolute (adj.) 绝对的 juéduìde

absolutely (adv.) 绝对地 juéduìde

absorb (v.) 吸收 xīshōu

abuse (n., v.) 虐待; 滥用 nüèdài; lànyòng

academic (adj.) 学术的 xuéshùde

academic term (n.) 学期 xuéqī

academic year (n.) 学年 xuénián

accelerate (v.) 加速 jiāsù

accent (n.) 口音 kǒuyīn

117

accept (v.) 接受 jiēshòu

acceptance (n.) 接受 jiēshòu

access (n.) 通路, 入门 tōnglù, rùmén

accessory (n.) 附件 fùjiàn

accident (n.) 事故 shìgù

accommodations (n.) 住处 zhùchù

accompany (v.) 陪同 péitóng

according to (prep.) 根据 gēnjù

account (n.) 账户, 陈述 zhànghù, chénshù

accountant (n.) 会计 kuàijì

accurate (adj.) 准确的 zhǔnquède

accuse (v.) 指控 zhǐkòng

accustom (v.) 使…习惯于 shǐ…xíguàn yú

ache (n.) 疼痛 téngtòng

achieve (v.) 取得 qǔdé

achievement (n.) 成就 chéngjiù

acknowledgement (n.) 承认, 鸣谢 chéngrèn, míngxiè

acquaintance (n.) 熟人 shúrén

acquire (v.) 获得 huòdé

across (prep.) 在…对面 zài…duìmiàn

act (n.) 动作 dòngzuò

action (n.) 行动 xíngdòng

active (adj.) 活跃的, 积极的 huóyuède, jījíde

activity (n.) 活动 huódòng

actor (n.) 演员 yǎnyuán

actress (n.) 女演员 nǚyǎnyuán

actually (adv.) 实际上 shíjìshang

adapt (v.) 使...适应 shǐ...shìyìng

add (v.) 加 jiā

addition (n.) 增加 zēngjiā

additional (adj.) 附加的, 额外的 fùjiāde, éwàide

address (n.) 地址 dìzhǐ

adjective (n.) 形容词 xíngróngcí

adjust (v.) 调整 tiáozhěng

administration (n.) 行政部门 xíngzhèng bùmén

admire (v.) 敬佩 jìngpèi

admission (n.) 接纳, 录取 jiēnà, lùqǔ

admission fee (n.) 入场费, 门票 rùchǎngfèi, ménpiào

admission ticket (n.) 入场券 rùchǎngquàn

admit (v.) 承认, 录取 chéngrèn, lùqǔ

adolescence (n.) 青春期 qīngchūnqī

adopt (v.) 收养, 采纳 shōuyǎng, cǎi'nà

adult (n.) 成人 chéngrén

adultery (n.) 通奸 tōngjiān

advance (n.) 前进, 预付款 qiánjìn, yùfùkuǎn

advantage (n.) 优势 yōushì

advantageous (adj.) 有利的 yǒulìde

adventure (n.) 历险 lìxiǎn

advertise (v.) 做广告 zuò guǎnggào

advertisement (n.) 广告 guǎnggào

advice (n.) 忠告 zhōnggào

advise (v.) 劝告 quàngào

affect (v.) 影响 yǐngxiǎng

afford (v.) 提供 tígòng

afraid (adj.) 害怕, 恐怕 hàipà, kǒngpà

Africa (n.) 非洲 fēizhōu

African (adj., n.) 非洲的; 非洲人 Fēizhōude;
   Fēizhōurén

after (prep., conj.) 在…之后 zài...zhīhòu

afternoon (n.) 下午 xiàwǔ

again (adv.) 再 zài

against (prep.) 反对 fǎnduì

age (n.) 年龄 niánlíng

agency (n.) 代理 dàilǐ

agent (n.) 代理商 dàilǐshāng

aggression (n.) 侵略 qīnlüè

aggressive (adj.) 好斗的 hàodòude

ago (adv.) 以前 yǐqián

agree (v.) 同意 tóngyì

agreement (n.) 协议 xiéyì

ahead (adv.) 在前面 zài qiánmian

aid (n.) 援助 yuánzhù

air (n.) 空气 kōngqì

air-conditioning (n.) 空调 kōngtiáo

airfare (n.) 飞机票价 fēijī piàojià

airline (n.) 航空公司 hángkōng gōngsī

airline ticket (n.) 机票 jīpiào

airmail (n.) 航空邮件 hángkōng yóujiàn

airplane (n.) 飞机 fēijī

airport (n.) 机场 jīchǎng

aisle (n.) 过道 guòdào

alarm (n.) 警报 jǐngbào

alarm clock (n.) 闹钟 nàozhōng

alcohol (n.) 酒精 jiǔjīng

alien (n.) 外侨 wàiqiáo

alike (adj.) 相似的 xiāngsìde

alive (adj.) 活着 huózhe

all (adj., adv.) 所有的; 全体 suǒyǒude; quántǐ

all right (id.) 好啊 hǎo a

allergic (adj.) 过敏 guòmǐn

allergy (n.) 过敏症 guòmǐnzhèng

allow (v.) 允许 yǔnxǔ

almost (adv.) 几乎 jīhū

alone (adv.) 独自 dúzì

aloud (adv.) 大声地 dàshēngde

alphabet (n.) 字母表 zìmǔbiǎo

already (adv.) 已经 yǐjing

also (adv.) 也 yě

although (conj.) 虽然 suīrán

altitude (n.) 海拔高度 hǎibá gāodù

altogether (adv.) 总共 zǒnggòng

always (adv.) 总是 zǒngshì

amaze (v.) 使…吃惊 shǐ...chījīng

ambassador (n.) 大使 dàshǐ

ambiguous (adj.) 模糊的 móhude

ambition (n.) 野心, 抱负 yěxīn, bàofù

ambulance (n.) 救护车 jiùhùchē

America (n.) 美国, 美洲 Měiguó, Měizhōu

American (n., adj.) 美国人; 美国的 Měiguórén; Měiguóde

among (prep.) 在…之中 zài...zhīzhōng

amount (n.) 数量 shùliàng

ancestor (n.) 祖先 zǔxiān

ancient (adj.) 古代的 gǔdàide

and (conj.) 和 hé

anemia (n.) 贫血 pínxuě

anesthesia (n.) 麻醉 mázuì

angel (n.) 天使 tiānshǐ

anger (n.) 气愤 qìfèn

angry (adj.) 愤怒 fènnù

animal (n.) 动物 dòngwù

ankle (n.) 脚腕 jiǎowàn

anniversary (n.) 周年 zhōunián

announcement (n.) 通知 tōngzhī

annual (adj.) 一年一次的 yì nián yí cì de

another (adj.) 另一 lìngyī

answer (n., v.) 答案; 回答 dá'àn; huídá

antenna (n.) 天线 tiānxiàn

antiquity (n.) 古代 gǔdài

anxiety (n.) 焦急 jiāojí

any (adj.) 任何 rènhé

anybody (pron.) 任何人 rènhérén

apart (adv.) 分开地 fēnkāide

apartment (n.) 公寓 gōngyù

apologize (v.) 道歉 dàoqiàn

appearance (n.) 出现, 外观 chūxiàn, wàiguān

appendicitis (n.) 阑尾炎 lánwěiyán

appetite (n.) 食欲, 胃口 shíyù, wèikǒu

appetizer (n.) 前菜, 冷盘 qiáncài, lěngpán

applaud (v.) 鼓掌 gǔzhǎng

applause (n.) 鼓掌 gǔzhǎng

apple (n.) 苹果 píngguǒ

appliance (n.) 用具（电器） yòngjù (diànqì)

application (n.) 申请 shēnqǐng

apply (v.) 申请 shēnqǐng

appointment (n.) 约会, 预约 yuēhuì, yùyuē

apprentice (n.) 学徒 xuétú

approach (n.) 途径, 方式 tújìng, fāngshì

appropriate (adj.) 适当的 shìdàngde

approve (v.) 赞成, 批准 zànchéng, pīzhǔn

April (n.) 四月 sìyuè

Arab (n.) 阿拉伯人 Alābórén

Arabic (n.) 阿拉伯语 Alābóyǔ

architecture (n.) 建筑 jiànzhù

archive (n.) 档案文件 dàng'àn wénjiàn

area (n.) 地区 dìqū

argument (n.) 争论 zhēnglùn

arm (n.) 手臂 shǒubì

armchair (n.) 扶手椅 fúshǒuyǐ

armpit (n.) 腋窝 yèwō

army (n.) 军队 jūnduì

around (adv., prep.) 周围; 在…周围 zhōuwéi; zài...zhōuwéi

arrest (n., v.) 逮捕 dǎibǔ

arrival (n.) 到达 dàodá

arrive (v.) 到达 dàodá

arrow (n.) 箭，箭头 jiàn, jiàntóu

art (n.) 艺术 yìshù

article (n.) 文章 wénzhāng

artificial (adj.) 人造的 rénzàode

artist (n.) 艺术家 yìshùjiā

as (conj., prep.) 当…时; 作为 dāng...shí; zuòwéi

ash (n.) 灰 huī

ashtray (n.) 烟灰缸 yānhuīgāng

Asia (n.) 亚洲 Yàzhōu

Asian (n., adj.) 亚洲人; 亚洲的 Yàzhōurén;
Yàzhōude

aside (adv.) 在旁边 zài pángbiān

ask (v.) 问 wèn

asleep (adj.) 熟睡的 shúshuìde

aspirin (n.) 阿司匹林 āsīpīlín

assemble (v.) 集合, 组装 jíhé, zǔzhuāng

assign (v.) 指派 zhǐpài

assist (v.) 协助 xiézhù

assistant (n.) 助手 zhùshǒu

association (n.) 协会 xiéhuì

assure (v.) 使（人）确信 shǐ (rén) quèxìn

asylum (n.) 收容所, 避难所 shōuróngsuǒ,
bì'nànsuǒ

at (prep.) 在 zài

athlete (n.) 运动员 yùndòngyuán

attempt (n., v.) 企图; 尝试 qǐtú; chángshì

attention (n.) 注意 zhùyì

attentive (adj.) 专心的 zhuānxīnde

attic (n.) 阁楼 gélóu

attitude (n.) 态度 tàidu

attorney (n.) 律师 lùshī

attract (v.) 吸引 xīyǐn

attractive (adj.) 吸引人的, 美貌的 xīyǐnrénde, měimàode

auction (n.) 拍卖 pāimài

August (n.) 八月 bāyuè

aunt (n.) 姑妈, 舅母, 阿姨 gūmā, jiùmu, āyí

authentic (adj.) 真实的, 道地的 zhēnshíde, dàodìde

author (n.) 作家, 作者 zuòjiā, zuòzhě

authority (n.) 权威 quánwēi

authorization (n.) 授权 shòuquán

authorize (v.) 授权 shòuquán

automatic (adj.) 自动的 zìdòngde

available (adj.) 可用的, 可有的 kěyòngde, kěyǒude

avenue (n.) 大道 dàdào

average (n.) 平均 píngjūn

avoid (v.) 避免 bìmiǎn

aware (adj.) 知道, 意识到 zhīdào, yìshidào

away (adv.) 在远处, 到远处 zài yuǎnchù, dào yuǎnchù

awful (adj.) 可怕的 kěpàde

B

baby (n.) 婴儿 yīng'ér

baby-sit (v.) 照管孩子 zhàoguǎn háizi

baby-sitter (n.) 保姆 bǎomǔ

bachelor (n.) 学士, 单身汉 xuéshì, dānshēnhàn

back (adv.) 在后面 zài hòumian

back (n.) 后背 hòubèi

backache (n.) 背痛 bèitòng

backbone (n.) 脊椎 jǐzhuī

backpack/knapsack (n.) 背包 bèibāo

backwards (adv.) 向后 xiànghòu

bacteria (n.) 细菌 xìjūn

bad (adj.) 坏的 huàide

bag (n.) 袋, 包 dài, bāo

baggage (n.) 行李 xíngli

bail (n.) 取保金 qǔbǎojīn

bait (n.) 诱饵 yòu'ěr

bake (v.) 烤 kǎo

baker (n.) 面包师 miànbāoshī

bakery (n.) 面包店 miànbāodiàn

balance (n.) 平衡, 结余 pínghéng, jiéyú

balcony (n.) 阳台 yángtái

bald (adj.) 秃的 tūde

ball (dancing) (n.) 舞会 wǔhuì

ball (in some sports) (n.) 球 qiú

ballet (n.) 芭蕾舞 bāléiwǔ

ballpoint pen (n.) 圆珠笔 yuánzhūbǐ

ballroom (n.) 舞厅 wǔtīng

bamboo (n.) 竹子 zhúzi

ban (n., v.) 禁止 jìnzhǐ

band (n.) 乐队 yuèduì

bandage (n.) 绷带 bēngdài

bank (n.) 银行, 河岸 yínháng, hé'àn

banker (n.) 银行家 yínhángjiā

banquet (n.) 宴会 yànhuì

baptism (n.) 浸洗礼 jìnxǐlǐ

baptize (v.) 施洗礼 shīxǐlǐ

bar (n.) 酒吧 jiǔbā

barber (n.) 理发师 lǐfàshī

bare (adj.) 赤裸的 chìluǒde

barefoot (adv.) 赤脚 chìjiǎo

bargain (v.) 议价, 讨价还价 yìjià, tǎojià huánjià

barn (n.) 谷仓, 畜棚 gǔcāng, xùpéng

baseball (n.) 棒球 bàngqiú

basement (n.) 地下室 dìxiàshì

basin (n.) 盆，盆地 pén, péndì

basis (n.) 基础 jīchǔ

basket (n.) 篮子 lánzi

basketball (n.) 篮球 lánqiú

bath (n.) 澡 xǐzǎo

bathe/take a bath (v.) 淋浴, 洗澡 línyù, xǐzǎo

bathing suit (n.) 游泳衣 yóuyǒngyī

bathrobe (n.) 浴衣 yùyī

bathroom (n.) 厕所 cèsuǒ

bathtub (n.) 浴缸 yùgāng

battery (n.) 电池 diànchí

bay (n.) 海湾 hǎiwān

be (v.) 是 shì

beach (n.) 海滩 hǎitān

bean (n.) 豆子 dòuzi

bear (n.) 熊 xióng

bear (v.) 忍受 rěnshòu

bearable (adj.) 可忍受的 kěrěnshòude

beard (n.) 胡须 húxū

beat (v.) 打 dǎ

beautiful (adj.) 美丽的 měilìde

beauty (n.) 美 měi

because (conj.) 因为 yīnwèi

become (v.) 成为 chéngwéi

bed (n.) 床 chuáng

bedding (n.) 寝具 qǐnjù

bedroom (n.) 卧室 wòshì

bee (n.) 蜜蜂 mìfēng

beef (n.) 牛肉 niúròu

beer (n.) 啤酒 píjiǔ

before (prep., conj.) 在…之前 zài...zhīqián

before (when telling time) (adv.) 以前 yǐqián

beg (v.) 乞求 qǐqiú

beggar (n.) 乞丐 qǐgài

begin (v.) 开始 kāishǐ

beginner (n.) 初学者 chūxuézhě

beginning (n.) 开始 kāishǐ

behave (v.) 表现 biǎoxiàn

behavior (n.) 行为 xíngwéi

behind (prep., conj.) 在…之后 zài...zhīhòu

Belgian (n.) 比利时人 Bǐlìshírén

Belgium (n.) 比利时 Bǐlìshí

belief (n.) 信仰, 信念 xìnyǎng, xìnniàn

believe (v.) 相信 xiāngxìn

bell (n.) 钟, 铃 zhōng, líng

bellboy, bellhop (n.) 旅馆服务员 lǚguǎn
    fúwùyuán

belly (n.) 肚子 dùzi

belong (v.) 属于 shǔyú

belongings (n.) 财物 cáiwù

below (prep.) 在…下面 zài...xiàmian

belt (n.) 带子 dàizi

bench (n.) 长凳 chángdèng

benefit (n.) 利益, 福利 lìyì,fúlì

beret (n.) 贝雷帽 bèiléimào

berry (n.) 浆果 jiāngguǒ

beside (prep.) 在…旁边 zài...pángbiān

besides (prep., adv.) 除…之外; 此外
    chú...zhīwài; cǐwài

best (adj.) 最好的 zuìhǎode

bet (n., v.) 赌, 打赌 dǔ, dǎdǔ

better (adj.) 更好的 gènghǎode

between (prep.) 在…之间 zài...zhījiān

beverage (n.) 饮料 yǐnliào

beware (v.) 小心 xiǎoxīn

beyond (prep.) 在…之外, 超出… zài...zhīwài, chāochū.

bib (n.) 围兜 wéidōu

Bible (n.) 圣经 shèngjīng

bicycle (n.) 自行车 zìxíngchē

big (adj.) 大的 dàde

bilingual (adj.) 双语的 shuāngyǔde

bill/check (at a restaurant) (n.) 帐单 zhàngdān

billion (n.) 十亿 shíyì

bird (n.) 鸟 niǎo

birth (n.) 出生 chūshēng

birth control pill (n.) 避孕丸 bìyùnwán

birthday (n.) 生日 shēngrì

bit (n.) 一小片, 一点儿 yìxiǎopiàn, yìdiǎnr

bite (v.) 咬 yǎo

bitter (adj.) 苦的 kǔde

black (adj.) 黑色的 hēisède

blackboard (n.) 黑板 hēibǎn

bladder (n.) 膀胱 pángguāng

blade (n.) 刀刃 dāorèn

blank (adj.) 空白的 kòngbáide

blanket (n.) 毯子 tǎnzi

bleach (v., n.) 漂白; 漂白剂 piǎobái; piǎobáijì

bleed (v.) 出血 chūxiě

blend (n.) 混合 hùnhé

bless (v.) 祝福 zhùfú

blind (adj.) 瞎的 xiāde

blindness (n.) 失明 shīmíng

blink (v. n.) 眨眼 zhǎyǎn

blister (n.) 水泡 shuǐpào

block (city block) (n.) 街区 jiēqū

blond (adj.) 金发的 jīnfàde

blouse (n.) 女式衬衫 nǚshì chènshān

blow-dry (n.) 吹干 chuī gān

blue (adj.) 蓝色的 lánsède

board (n.) 木板, 董事会 mùbǎn, dǒngshìhuì

boarding pass (n.) 登机牌 dēngjīpái

boarding school (n.) 寄宿学校 jìsù xuéxiào

boat (n.) 船 chuán

body (n.) 身体 shēntǐ

boil (v.) 煮 zhǔ

bolt (n.) 插销, 螺栓 chāxiāo, luóshuān

bomb (n., v.) 炸弹; 轰炸 zhàdàn; hōngzhà

bone (n.) 骨头 gǔtou

book (n.) 书 shū

bookcase (n.) 书架 shūjià

bookstore (n.) 书店 shūdiàn

boot (n.) 靴子 xuēzi

border (n.) 边界 biānjiè

born (adj.) 出生 chūshēng

borrow (v.) 借 jiè

boss (n.) 老板 lǎobǎn

both (adj., pron.) 两者 liǎngzhě

bother (v.) 打扰 dǎrǎo

bottle (n.) 瓶子 píngzi

boulevard (n.) 林荫大道 línyìn dàdào

bow (n.) 弓 gōng

bowl (n.) 碗 wǎn

box (n.) 盒子 hézi

boxing (n.) 拳击 quánjī

boyfriend (n.) 男朋友 nánpéngyou

bra (n.) 胸罩 xiōngzhào

bracelet (n.) 手镯 shǒuzhuó

Brazil (n.) 巴西 Bāxī

Brazilian (n., adj.) 巴西人; 巴西的 Bāxīrén;
    Bāxīde

bread (n.) 面包 miànbāo

break (n., v.) 休息; 打破 xiūxi; dǎpò

break (take a break) (id.) 休息一下, 小憩
    xiūxiyíxià, xiǎoqì

breakdown (n.) 故障 gùzhàng

breakfast (n.) 早餐 zǎocān

breast (n.) 乳房 rǔfáng

breath (n.) 呼吸 hūxī

breathe (v.) 呼吸 hūxī

breeze (n.) 微风 wēifēng

bride (n.) 新娘 xīnniáng

bridge (n.) 桥 qiáo

brief (adj.) 简短的 jiǎnduǎnde

bright (adj.) 明亮的 míngliàngde

bring (v.) 带来 dài lái

broken (adj.) 坏了的 huài le de

broom (n.) 扫帚 sàozhou

brother (older) (n.) 哥哥 gēge

brother (younger) (n.) 弟弟 dìdi

brother-in-law (n.) 姐夫, 妹夫, 内兄, 内弟 jiěfu, mèifu, nèixiōng, nèidì

brown (adj.) 棕色的 zōngsède

bruise (n., v.) 青肿; 撞伤 qīngzhǒng; zhuàng shāng

brush (n., v.) 刷; 刷子 shuā; shuāzi

bubble (n.) 水泡, 气泡 shuǐpào, qìpào

bucket (n.) 桶 tǒng

Buddhism (n.) 佛教 fójiào

Buddhist (n.) 佛教徒 fójiàotú

budget (n.) 预算 yùsuàn

build (v.) 建造 jiànzào

building (n.) 建筑, 楼 jiànzhù, lóu

bulb (n.) 灯泡 dēngpào

bullet (n.) 子弹 zǐdàn

bunch (n.) 束 shù

burglar (n.) 小偷 xiǎotōu

burglarize (v.) 盗窃 dàoqiè

burn (n., v.) 烧伤; 烧 shāo shāng; shāo

burst (v.) 爆裂, 破裂 bàoliè, pòliè

bury (v.) 掩埋 yǎnmái

bus (n.) 公共汽车 gōnggòng qìchē

bus station (n.) 公交车站 gōngjiāochēzhàn

business (n.) 商业, 生意 shāngyè, shēngyì

businessperson (n.) 商人 shāngrén

busy (adj.) 忙 máng

but (conj.) 但是 dànshì

butcher (n.) 屠夫 túfū

butter (n.) 奶油 nǎiyóu

button (n.) 纽扣 niǔkòu

buy (v.) 买 mǎi

by (a means of transport) (prep.) 乘 chéng

by the way (id.) 顺便说 shùnbiàn shuō

bye (interj.) 再见 zàijiàn

bye-bye! (interj.) 再见! zàijiàn!

C

cab (n.) 出租车 chūzūchē

cable (n.) 电缆 diànlǎn

cable TV (n.) 有线电视 yǒuxiàn diànshì

café (n.) 咖啡馆 kāfēiguǎn

cage (n.) 笼子 lóngzi

cake (n.) 蛋糕 dàn'gāo

calculate (v.) 计算 jìsuàn

calculator (n.) 计算器 jìsuànqì

calendar (n.) 日历 rìlì

call (make a phone call) (v.) 打电话 dǎ
    diànhuà

call back (v.) 回电话 huí diànhuà

calling card (n.) 电话卡 diànhuàkǎ

camera (n.) 照像机 zhàoxiàngjī

camp (n.) 营地 yíngdì

can (aux.) 可以, 能 kěyǐ, néng

Canada (n.) 加拿大 Jiānádà

Canadian (n., adj.) 加拿大人; 加拿大的
    Jiānádàrén; Jiānádàde

cancel (v.) 取消 qǔxiāo

cancellation (n.) 取消 qǔxiāo

cancer (n.) 癌症 áizhèng

candle (n.) 蜡烛 làzhú

candy (n.) 糖果 tángguǒ

cane (n.) 手杖 shǒuzhàng

canoe (n.) 独木舟 dúmùzhōu

capable (adj.) 有能力的 yǒunénglìde

capital (city) (n.) 首都 shǒudū

capital (money) (n.) 资本 zīběn

captain (n.) 船长, 球队队长 chuánzhǎng, qiúduì duìzhǎng

car (n.) 轿车 jiàochē

cardboard (n.) 硬纸板 yìngzhǐbǎn

cards (n.) 卡片 kǎpiàn

care (n.) 忧虑, 关心 yōulù, guānxīn

care (take good care of) (id.) 精心照顾 jīngxīn zhàogù

careful(ly) (adj., adv.) 小心的; 仔细地 xiǎoxīnde; zǐxìde

carry (v.) 携带 xiédài

carton (n.) 纸盒, 纸箱 zhǐhé, zhǐxiāng

case (n.) 个案, 案例, 箱子 gè'àn, ànlì, xiāngzi

cash (n.) 现金 xiànjīn

cashier (n.) 收款员 shōukuǎnyuán

casino (n.) 赌场 dǔchǎng

casual (adj.) 随便的 suíbiànde

cat (n.) 猫 māo

catalog (n.) 目录 mùlù

catch (v.) 抓 zhuā

catch a train/bus (v.) 赶车 gǎnchē

cathedral (n.) 大教堂 dàjiàotáng

Catholic (n., adj.) 天主教徒; 天主教的 Tiānzhǔjiàotú; Tiānzhǔjiàode

cause (n., v.) 引起; 原因 yǐnqǐ; yuányīn

caution (v; n.) 告诫; 警告, 谨慎 gàojiè; jǐnggào, jǐnshèn

cautious (adj.) 谨慎的, 小心的 jǐnshènde, xiǎoxīnde

cave (n.) 山洞 shāndòng

ceiling (n.) 天花板 tiānhuābǎn

celebrate (v.) 庆祝 qìngzhù

cell (n.) 细胞 xìbāo

cell phone (n.) 手机 shǒujī

cellar (n.) 地窖 dìjiào

cemetery (n.) 墓地 mùdì

center (n.) 中心 zhōngxīn

centimeter (n.) 厘米 límǐ

central (adj.) 中心的 zhōngxīnde

century (n.) 世纪 shìjì

ceremony (n.) 典礼 diǎnlǐ

certain (adj.) 必然的, 一定的 bìránde, yídìngde

chain (n.) 链子 liànzi

chair (n.) 椅子, 主席 yǐzi, zhǔxí

champagne (n.) 香槟酒 xiāngbīnjiǔ

chance (n.) 机会 jīhuì

change (n., v.) 换; 变化 huàn; biànhuà

chapter (n.) 章（节）zhāng(jié)

character (n.) 人物, 人格 rénwù, réngé

chat (n., v.) 聊天 liáotiān

cheap (adj.) 便宜的 piányide

cheat (v.) 欺骗, 作弊 qīpiàn, zuòbì

check (n.) 支票 zhīpiào

check (at a restaurant) (n.) 帐单 zhàngdān

checkbook (n.) 支票本 zhīpiàoběn

checkroom (n.) 衣帽间 yīmàojiān

cheek (n.) 面颊 miànjiá

cheerful (adj.) 愉快的 yúkuàide

cheers! (interj.) 干杯! gānbēi!

cheese (n.) 奶酪 nǎilào

chef (n.) 厨师 chúshī

chemical (n., adj.) 化学品; 化学的 huàxuépǐn; huàxuéde

chemist (n.) 化学家 huàxuéjiā

chemistry (n.) 化学 huàxué

chess (n.) 国际象棋 guójì xiàngqí

chest (n.) 胸 xiōng

chew (v.) 嚼 jiáo

chicken (n.) 鸡 jī

child/children (n.) 儿童 értóng

childhood (n.) 童年 tóngnián

chin (n.) 下颚 xià'è

China (n.) 中国 Zhōngguó

Chinese (n., adj.) 中国人, 中文; 中国的
　　Zhōngguórén, Zhōngwén; Zhōngguóde

choice (n.) 选择 xuǎnzé

choke (v.) 哽噎 gěngyē

choose (v.) 选择 xuǎnzé

chop (v.) 剁, 砍 duò, kǎn

chopstick(s) (n.) 筷子 kuàizi

chore (n.) 杂务 záwù

Christian (n., adj.) 基督徒; 基督教的 Jīdūtú;
　　Jīdūjiàode

Christianity (n.) 基督教 Jīdūjiào

Christmas (n.) 圣诞节 Shèngdànjié

church (n.) 教堂 jiàotáng

cigar (n.) 雪茄 xuějiā

cigarette (n.) 香烟 xiāngyān

circle (n.) 圆圈 yuánquān

circumstance (n.) 状况, 环境 zhuàngkuàng,
　　huánjìng

circus (n.) 马戏团 mǎxìtuán

citizen (n.) 公民 gōngmín

city (n.) 城市 chéngshì

civilization (n.) 文明 wénmíng

class (school) (n.) 班级 bānjí

classic (adj.) 古典的 gǔdiǎnde

clean (adj.) 清洁的 qīngjiéde

clear(ly) (adj., adv.) 清楚的; 清楚地
　　qīngchǔde; qīngchǔde

clever (adj.) 聪明的 cōngmingde

client (n.) 客户 kèhù

cliff (n.) 悬崖 xuányá

climate (n.) 气候 qìhòu

climb (v.) 爬 pá

clinic (n.) 诊所 zhěnsuǒ

clock (n.) 钟 zhōng

close (v.) 关 guān

close (near in friendship) (adj.) 亲近的
　　qīnjìnde

closed (adj.) 关闭的 guānbìde

cloth (n.) 布 bù

clothes (n.) 衣服 yīfu

cloud (n.) 云 yún

coast (n.) 海岸 hǎi'àn

coat (n.) 大衣 dàyī

code (n.) 密码, 代号 mìmǎ, dàihào

coffee (n.) 咖啡 kāfēi

coffee shop (n.) 咖啡馆 kāfēiguǎn

coffin (n.) 棺材 guāncai

coin (n.) 硬币 yìngbì

cold (adj.) 冷 lěng

cold (sickness) (n.) 感冒 gǎnmào

colleague (n.) 同事 tóngshì

collect call (n.) 对方付费电话 duìfāng fùfèi diànhuà

collection (n.) 收集 shōují

college (n.) 学院 xuéyuàn

collide (v.) 碰撞 pèngzhuàng

collision (n.) 碰撞 pèngzhuàng

color (n.) 颜色 yánsè

column (n.) 专栏 zhuānlán

comb (n.) 梳子 shūzi

combination (n.) 综合 zōnghé

come (v.) 来 lái

comfortable (adj.) 舒适的 shūshìde

comforter (n.) 被子 bèizi

comma (n.) 逗号 dòuhào

comment (n.) 评论, 意见 pínglùn, yìjian

commission (n.) 佣金 yòngjīn

committee (n.) 委员会 wěiyuánhuì

common (adj.) 共同的, 普通的 gòngtóngde, pǔtōngde

communicate (v.) 交际 jiāojì

communications (n.) 通讯 tōngxùn

company (n.) 公司 gōngsī

compare (v.) 比较 bǐjiào

comparison (n.) 比较 bǐjiào

compartment (n.) 车厢 chēxiāng

compass (n.) 指南针 zhǐ'nánzhēn

compensate (v.) 补偿 bǔcháng

competence (n.) 能力 nénglì

competition (n.) 比赛 bǐsài

complain (v.) 抱怨 bàoyuàn

complaint (n.) 抱怨, 诉苦 bàoyuàn, sùkǔ

complete (adj., v.) 完整的; 完成 wánzhěngde;
    wánchéng

completion (n.) 完成 wánchéng

complicate (v.) 使...复杂 shǐ...fùzá

complicated (adj.) 复杂的 fùzáde

compliment (n.) 称赞 chēngzàn

comply (v.) 答应, 顺从 dāying, shùncóng

compose (v.) 写作 xiězuò

composition (n.) 作文 zuòwén

comprehensive (adj.) 综合的, 全面的
    zōnghéde, quánmiànde

computer (n.) 电脑 diànnǎo

concern (n.) 关心, 忧虑 guānxīn, yōulǜ

concert (n.) 音乐会 yīnyuèhuì

concrete (adj.) 具体的 jùtǐde

condemn (v.) 谴责 qiǎnzé

condition (n.) 情况, 条件 qíngkuàng, tiáojiàn

condolences (n.) 哀悼 āidào

condom (n.) 避孕套 bìyùntào

conductor (n.) 乐队指挥, 公共汽车售票员
    yuèduì zhǐhuī; gōnggòng qìchē
    shòupiàoyuán

conference (n.) 会议 huìyì

confess (v.) 坦白 tǎnbái

confession (n.) 坦白 tǎnbái

confidence (n.) 信心 xìnxīn

confirm (v.) 确认 quèrèn

conflict (n., v.) 冲突 chōngtū

confuse (v.) 混淆 hùnxiáo

congratulate (v.) 祝贺 zhǔhè

congratulations (interj.) 祝贺你 zhùhè nǐ

connect (v.) 联结 liánjié

connection (n.) 联结, 联系, 关系 liánjié, liánxì, guānxì

conscious (adj.) 有意识的 yǒuyìshíde

consequence (n.) 后果 hòuguǒ

conserve (v.) 保存 bǎocún

consider (v.) 考虑 kǎolǜ

consonant (n.) 辅音 fǔyīn

constipation (n.) 便秘 biànmì

construction (n.) 建设, 结构 jiànshè, jiégòu

consul (n.) 领事 lǐngshì

consulate (n.) 领事馆 lǐngshìguǎn

contact (n., v.) 接触; 联系 jiēchù; liánxì

contact lenses (n.) 隐形眼镜 yǐnxíng yǎnjìng

contagious (adj.) 传染性的 chuánrǎnxìngde

contain (v.) 包含 bāohán

container (n.) 容器 róngqì

contaminate (v.) 污染 wūrǎn

contempt (n.) 藐视 miǎoshì

content (adj., n.) 满意的; 内容 mǎnyìde; nèiróng

continent (n.) 大陆, 陆地 dàlù, lùdì

continue (v.) 继续 jìxù

contraceptive (n.) 避孕用具 bìyùn yòngjù

contract (n.) 合同 hétong

contrary (n., adj.) 反面; 相反的 fǎnmiàn; xiāngfǎnde

control (n., v.) 控制 kòngzhì

convenient (adj.) 方便的 fāngbiànde

convent (n.) 女修道院 nǚxiūdàoyuàn

conversation (n.) 会话, 交谈 huìhuà, jiāotán

convert (v.) 转换, 兑换 zhuǎnhuàn, duìhuàn

convertible (adj.) 可转换的 kězhuǎnhuànde

convince (v.) 使...确信, 使...信服 shǐ...quèxìn, shǐ...xìnfú

cook (n.) 厨师 chúshī

cook (v.) 烹调, 做饭 pēngtiáo, zuòfàn

cooker (n.) 炊具 chuī_jù

cool (adj.) 凉爽的 liángshuǎngde

copy (n., v.) 副本; 抄写 fùběn; chāoxiě

copymachine (n.) 复印机 fùyìnjī

cord (n.) 绳索 shéngsuǒ

cordless (adj.) 无绳（电话） wúshéng (diànhuà)

core (n.) 核心, 果核 héxīn; guǒhú

cork (n.) 瓶塞 píngsāi

corner (n.) 角落, 街角 jiǎoluò, jiējiǎo

corporation (n.) 公司 gōngsī

corpse (n.) 尸体 shītǐ

correct (right) (adj.) 正确的 zhèngquède

correction (n.) 更正 gēngzhèng

correspondence (n.) 通信 tōngxìn

cost (n., v.) 成本, 费用; 耗费 chéngběn, fèiyòng; hàofèi

cot (n.) 帆布床 fānbùchuáng

cotton (n.) 棉花 miánhua

couch (n.) 长沙发 cháng shāfā

cough (n., v.) 咳嗽 késou

count (v.) 数 shǔ

counter (n.) 柜台 guìtái

country (n.) 国家, 乡村 guójiā, xiāngcūn

countryside (n.) 农村 nóngcūn

couple (n.) 夫妻, 一对 fūqī, yíduì

course (n.) 课程, 过程 kèchéng, guòchéng

court (n.) 法庭 fǎtíng

courteous(ly) (adj., adv.) 谦恭的; 有礼地 qiāngōngde; yǒulǐde

courtyard (n.) 院子 yuànzi

cousin (n.) 堂哥, 堂弟, 堂姐, 堂妹, 表哥, 表弟, 表姐, 表妹 tánggē, tángdì, tángjiě, tángmèi, biǎogē, biǎodì, biǎojiě, biǎomèi

cover (n., v.) 封面; 盖 fēngmiàn; gài

cow (n.) 牛 niú

cozy (adj.) 舒适的 shūshìde

crab (n.) 螃蟹 pángxiè

crack (n., v.) 裂缝; 破裂 lièfèng; pòliè

cradle (n.) 摇篮 yáolán

craft (n.) 工艺, 手艺 gōngyì, shǒuyì

craftsman (n.) 工匠 gōngjiàng

crash (n., v.) 坠毁; 碰撞 zhuìhuǐ; pèngzhuàng

crawl (v.) 爬 pá

crazy (adj.) 疯狂的 fēngkuángde

cream (n.) 奶油 nǎiyóu

create (v.) 创造 chuàngzào

credit card (n.) 信用卡 xìnyòngkǎ

crew (n.) 全体机务人员, 全体船员 quántǐ jīwù rényuán, quántǐ chuányuán

crime (n.) 犯罪 fànzuì

criticism (n.) 批评 pīpíng

criticize (v.) 批评 pīpíng

crop (n.) 庄稼 zhuāngjia

cross (n., v.) 十字架; 穿过 shízìjià; chuānguò

crossing (n.) 人行道, 十字路口 rénxíngdào, shízìlùkǒu

crowd (n.) 人群 rénqún

crowded (adj.) 拥挤的 yōngjǐde

cruise (n., v.) 航游 hángyóu

crumb (n.) 碎屑 suìxiè

crumble (v.) 崩溃 bēngkuì

crust (n.) 硬皮 yìngpí

crutch (n.) 拐杖 guǎizhàng

cry (v.) 哭, 喊 kū, hǎn

cuddle (v.) 搂抱, 依偎 lǒubào, yīwēi

cuff (n.) 袖口 xiùkǒu

culture (n.) 文化 wénhuà

cup (n.) 杯子 bēizi

cupboard (n.) 碗橱 wǎnchú

cure (n.) 治愈 zhìyù

curious (adj.) 好奇的 hàoqíde

curl (v.) 卷曲 juǎnqū

currency (n.) 货币 huòbì

current (adj.) 目前的 mùqiánde

curtain (n.) 帘子 liánzi

curve (n.) 曲线 qūxiàn

cushion (n.) 坐垫 zuòdiàn

custom (n.) 习俗 xísú

customer (n.) 顾客 gùkè

customs(atanairport) (n.) 海关 hǎiguān

cut (v.) 切, 割 qiē, gē

cute (adj.) 可爱的 kě'àide

D

daily (adj.) 每日的, 日常的 měirìde, rìchángde

dance (n., v.) 舞蹈; 跳舞 wǔdǎo; tiàowǔ

dangerous (adj.) 危险的 wēixiǎnde

dark (adj.) 黑暗的 hēi'ànde

daughter (n.) 女儿 nǚér

daughter-in-law (n.) 媳妇 xífù

day (n.) 天, 日子 tiān, rìzi

December (n.) 十二月 shí'èryuè

decide (v.) 决定 juédìng

definitely (adv.) 确切地 quèqiède

degree (diploma) (n.) 学位 xuéwèi

degree (temperature) (n.) 度 dù

delicious (adj.) 好吃的 hǎochīde

deliver (v.) 送 (货) song (huò)

dentist (n.) 牙医 yáyī

depart (v.) 离开, 出发 líkāi, chūfā

department (at a college) (n.) 系 xì

department chair (n.) 系主任 xì zhǔrèn

dependable (adj.) 可靠的 kěkàode

deposit (v., n.) 存款; 押金 cúnkuǎn; yājīn

descendant (n.) 后代 hòudài

devastate (v.) 毁坏 huǐhuài

develop (v.) 发展 fāzhǎn

development (n.) 发展 fāzhǎn

dialogue (n.) 对话 duìhuà

dictionary (n.) 字典 zìdiǎn

die (v.) 死 sǐ

different (adj.) 不同的 bùtóngde

difficult (adj.) 困难的 kùnnánde

diligent (adj.) 勤勉的 qínmiǎnde

dining table (n.) 餐桌 cānzhuō

dinner (n.) 晚餐 wǎncān

diplomat (n.) 外交官 wàijiāoguān

direct (give directions) (v.) 指挥, 指路 zhǐhuī, zhǐlù

directions (n.) 方向 fāngxiàng

director (of a company) (n.) 主任 zhǔrèn

director (of a movie) (n.) 导演 dǎoyǎn

dirty (adj.) 脏的 zāngde

disabled (adj.) 伤残的 shāngcánde

disagree (v.) 不同意 bù tóngyì

disappointed (adj.) 失望的 shīwàngde

disaster (n.) 灾难 zāinàn

discusion (n.) 讨论 tǎolùn

discuss (v.) 讨论 tǎolùn

disease (n.) 疾病 jíbìng

dish (a container) (n.) 盘子 pánzi

dish (of food) (n.) 菜 cài

district (n.) 区 qū

divorced (adj.) 离婚的 líhūnde

dizzy (adj.) 眩晕 xuányūn

do (v.) 做 zuò

doctor (n.) 医生 yīshēng

doctor's office (n.) 诊所 zhěnsuǒ

dog (n.) 狗 gǒu

dollar (n.) 美元 měiyuán

door (n.) 门 mén

dormitory (n.) 宿舍 sùshè

double room (n.) 双人间 shuāngrénjiān

down (adv.) 下 xià

downstairs (adv.) 在楼下, 往楼下 zài lóuxià, wǎng lóuxià

dress (v.) 穿衣 chuānyī

dress (n.) 连衣裙 liányīqún

drink (v.) 喝 hē

drive (a car) (v.) 开 (车) kāi (chē)

drug (as in "drug addiction") (n.) 毒品 dúpǐn

drug (medicine) (n.) 药 yào

drunk (adj.) 喝醉的 hēzuìde

dry (adj.) 干的 gānde

dry-clean (v.) 干洗 gānxǐ

dryer (n.) 烘干机 hōnggānjī

during (prep.) 在…期间 zài...qījiān

duty-free (adj.) 免税的 miǎnshuìde

E

each (adj.) 各 gè

early (adj., adv.) 早 zǎo

earn (a salary) (v.) 挣 zhèng

earring(s) (n.) 耳环 ěrhuán

east (n.) 东方, 东部 dōngfāng, dōngbù

eastern (adj.) 东方的 dōngfāngde

easy (adj.) 容易的 róngyìde

eat (v.) 吃 chī

economics (n.) 经济学 jīngjìxué

economy (n.) 经济 jīngjì

editor (n.) 编辑 biānjí

education (n.) 教育 jiàoyù

egg (n.) 蛋 dàn

electricity (n.) 电 diàn

elementary (level) (adj.) 初级的 chūjíde

elementary school (n.) 小学 xiǎoxué

elevator (n.) 电梯 diàntī

embarrassed (adj.) 难为情的 nánwéiqíngde

embassy (n.) 大使馆 dàshǐguǎn

embroidery (n.) 刺绣 cìxiù

emergency (n.) 紧急情况 jǐnjí qíngkuàng.

employee (n.) 雇员 gùyuán

empty (adj.) 空的 kōngde

encourage (v.) 鼓励 gǔlì

end (n., v.) 结束 jiéshù

engaged to be married (adj.) 订了婚的 dìng le hūnde

engine (n.) 发动机 fādòngjī

English (language) (n.) 英文, 英语 Yīngwén, Yīngyǔ

English (teach English) (v.) 教英语 jiāo Yīngyǔ

enjoy (v.) 享受 xiǎngshòu

enjoyable (adj.) 令人愉快的 lìngrényúkuàide

enough (adj.) 足够的 zúgòude

enter (v.) 进入 jìnrù

entrance (n.) 入口 rùkǒu

envelope (n.) 信封 xìnfēng

equal (adj.) 相等的, 平等的 xiāngděngde, píngděngde

ethnic minority (n.) 少数民族 shǎoshù mínzú

evening (n.) 晚上 wǎnshang

everyday (n.) 每天 měi tiān

everyone (pron.) 每个人 měi ge rén

everything (pron.) 一切 yíqiè

everywhere (adv.) 到处 dàochù

exam (take an exam [school]) (v.) 考试 kǎoshì

examination (n.) 考试 kǎoshì

exchange money (v.) 换钱 huànqián

excuse me (id.) 对不起 duìbuqǐ

exercise (n., v.) 练习; 锻炼 liànxí; duànliàn

exhibition (n.) 展览 zhǎnlǎn

exit (n.) 出口 chūkǒu

expensive (adj.) 贵的 guìde

explain (v.) 解释 jiěshì

export (v.) 出口 chūkǒu

eye (n.) 眼睛 yǎnjing

eyeglasses (n.) 眼镜 yǎnjìng

F

fabric (n.) 布, 料子 bù, liàozi

face (n.) 脸 liǎn

factory (n.) 工厂 gōngchǎng

fall (autumn) (n.) 秋天 qiūtiān

fall (of people) (v.) 跌倒, 摔倒 diē dǎo, shuāi dǎo

fall (of things) (v.) 落下 luò xià

family (n.) 家庭 jiātíng

famous (adj.) 有名的 yǒumíngde

far (from) (adj.) 远 yuǎn

fare (air, train, etc.) (n.) 旅费 lǚfèi

farm (n.) 农场 nóngchǎng

fast (adj.) 快的 kuàide

fat (adj.) 胖的 pàngde

father (n.) 父亲 fùqin

father-in-law (n.) 岳父, 公公 yuèfù, gōnggong

feast (n.) 宴会 yànhuì

February (n.) 二月 èryuè

feed (v.) 喂 wèi

feel (v.) 感觉 gǎnjué

feeling (n.) 感觉, 感情 gǎnjué, gǎnqíng

festival (n.) 节日 jiérì

festive (adj.) 喜庆的 xǐqìngde

fever (n.) 发烧 fāshāo

field (paddy) (n.) 田 tián

film (n.) 电影, 胶卷 diànyǐng, jiāojuǎn

finance (n.) 财政 cáizhèng

financial (adj.) 金融的 jīnróngde

find (v.) 找到 zhǎo dào

finish (v.) 结束 jiéshù

fire (n.) 火 huǒ

first (adj.) 第一 dìyī

first-class (adj.) 一等 yīděng

fish (n.) 鱼 yú

fish sauce (n.) 鱼露 yúlù

fisherman (n.) 渔民 yúmín

fit (v.) 适合 shìhé

fix (v.) 修理 xiūlǐ

155

flashlight (n.) 手电筒 shǒudiàntǒng

flight (of planes) (n.) 航班 hángbān

flood (n.) 水灾, 洪水 shuǐzāi, hóngshuǐ

floor (in a hotel, etc.) (n.) 楼, 层 lóu, céng

flower (n.) 花 huā

fluent(ly) (adj., adv.) 流利的; 流利地 liúlìde; liúlìde

fly (take a plane) (v.) 坐飞机 zuò fēijī

folk song (n.) 民歌 míngē

follow (v.) 跟随, 遵循 gēnsuí, zūnxún

food (n.) 食物 shíwù

football (soccer) (n.) 足球 zúqiú

for (prep.) 为了, 给 wèile, gěi

foreign (adj.) 外国的 wàiguó

foreigner (n.) 外国人 wàiguórén

forest (n.) 森林 sēnlín

forget (v.) 忘记 wàngjì

fork (n.) 叉子 chāzi

formal (adj.) 正式的 zhèngshìde

fragrant (adj.) 芬芳的 fēnfāngde

free (free of charge) (adj.) 免费的 miǎnfèide

fresh (adj.) 新鲜的 xīnxiānde

friend (n.) 朋友 péngyou

friendly (adj.) 友好的 yǒuhǎode

friendship (n.) 友谊 yǒuyì

from (prep.) 从 cóng

fruit (n.) 水果 shuǐguǒ

fry (v.) 油炸 yóuzhà

full (adj.) 满的 mǎnde

full (cannot eat anymore) (adj.) 饱的 bǎode

full-time (adj.) 全职的 quánzhíde

fun (n., adj.) 乐趣; 有意思 lèqù; yǒuyìsi

funeral (n.) 葬礼 zànglǐ

future (n.) 未来 wèilái

G

garbage (n.) 垃圾 lājī

garden (n.) 花园 huāyuán

gas/petrol (n.) 汽油 qìyóu

general(ly) (adj., adv.) 一般的; 一般地 yībānde; yībānde

generous (adj.) 慷慨的 kāngkǎide

get (v.) 得到 dédào

get married (v.) 结婚 jiéhūn

get off (a bus) (v.) 下车 xià chē

get on (a bus) (v.) 上车 shàng chē

get up (v.) 起床 qǐchuáng

get-together (n., v.) 聚会 jùhuì

gift (n.) 礼物 lǐwù

girl (n.) 女孩 nǚhái

girlfriend (n.) 女朋友 nǚpéngyou

give (v.) 给 gěi

give (sb.) a hand (id.) 帮 bāng

glad (adj.) 高兴 gāoxìng

glass (drinking) (n.) 杯子 bēizi

go (v.) 去 qù

go home (v.) 回家 huíjiā

go into (v.) 进入 jìnrù

go out (v.) 出门 chūmén

go to a doctor (v.) 看医生 kàn yīshēng

go to bed (v.) 上床 shàngchuáng

go to school (v.) 上学 shàngxué

go to the movies (v.) 看电影 kàn diànyǐng

go to work (v.) 上班 shàngbān

gold (n.) 黄金 huángjīn

golf (n.) 高尔夫球 gāoěrfūqiú

good (adj.) 好 hǎo

good-bye (id.) 再见 zàijiàn

grade (n.) 年级, 分数 niánjí, fēnshù

graduate (v.) 毕业 bìyè

grandchild (n.) 孙辈 sūnbèi

grandfather (n.) 祖父, 外祖父 zǔfù, wàizǔfù

grandmother (n.) 祖母, 外婆 zǔmǔ, wàipó

grandparents (n.) 祖父母, 外祖父母 zǔfùmǔ, wàizǔfùmǔ

grandson/granddaughter (n.) 孙子, 孙女, 外孙, 外孙女 sūnzi, sūnnǚ, wàisūn, wàisūnnǚ green (adj.) 绿色的 lǜsède

greet (v.) 打招呼 dǎ zhāohu

greeting (n.) 致意 zhìyì

grill (v.) 烧烤 shāokǎo

groom (n.) 新郎 xīnláng

group (n.) 团, 组 tuán,zǔ

grow up (v.) 长大 zhǎngdà

guarantee (n., v.) 担保; 保证 dānbǎo; bǎozhèng

guess (n., v.) 猜测 cāicè

guest (n.) 客人 kèrén

guide (n.) 导游, 向导 dǎoyóu, xiàngdǎo

guitar (n.) 吉它 jítā

H

hair (n.) 头发 tóufa

haircut (n.) 理发 lǐfà

half (n.) 一半 yíbàn

half an hour (id.) 半小时 bàn xiǎoshí

halfway (adv.) 半路上 bànlùshang

hallway (n.) 走廊 zǒuláng

hand (n.) 手 shǒu

handicraft (n.) 手工艺 shǒugōngyì

handmade (adj.) 手工制作的 shǒugōng zhìzuòde

handsome (adj.) 英俊的 yīngjùnde

hang up (the phone) (v.) 挂 (电话) guà (diànhuà)

happiness (n.) 幸福 xìngfú

happy (adj.) 快乐的 kuàilède

hard (diligently) (adv.) 努力 nǔlì

hard (of objects) (adj.) 硬的 yìngde

harvest (n.) 收获 shōuhuò

hat (n.) 帽子 màozi

hate (v.) 恨 hèn

have (v.) 有 yǒu

he (pron.) 他 tā

head (n.) 头 tóu

headache (n.) 头痛 tóutòng

health (healthcare system) (n.) 医疗 yīliáo

health (of a person) (n.) 健康 jiànkāng

healthy (adj.) 健康的 jiànkāngde

hear (v.) 听到 tīngdào

heavily (regarding rain) (adv.) 大 dà

heavy (adj.) 重的 zhòngde

hello (interj.) 你好 nǐhǎo!

help (n., v.) 帮助 bāngzhù

her (pron.) 她 tā

here (adv.) 这里, 这儿 zhèlǐ, zhèr

high (adj.) 高 gāo

high school (n.) 高中 gāozhōng

hike (v.) 远足 yuǎnzú

his (pron.) 他的 tāde

history (n.) 历史 lìshǐ

hold (v.) 拿 ná

holiday (n.) 假日 jiàrì

home (n.) 家 jiā

homemaker (n.) 主妇 zhǔfù

honest (adj.) 诚实的 chéngshíde

honeymoon (n.) 蜜月 mìyuè

honored (adj.) 尊敬的 zūnjìngde

hope (n., v.) 希望 xīwàng

hospitable (adj.) 好客的 hàokède

hospital (n.) 医院 yīyuàn

hostel (n.) 客栈 kèzhàn

hot (adj.) 热的 rède

hotel (n.) 旅馆 lǚguǎn

hour (n.) 小时 xiǎoshí

house (n.) 房子 fángzi

how long (ques.) 多长 duō cháng

how many/much (ques.) 多少 duōshao

hug (n., v.) 拥抱 yōngbào

hundred (n.) 百 bǎi

hungry (adj.) 饥饿的 jī'ède

hurry (n., v.) 抓紧; 匆忙 zhuājǐn; cōngmáng

husband (n.) 丈夫 zhàngfu

I

I (pron.) 我 wǒ

ice (n.) 冰 bīng

ice cream (n.) 冰淇淋 bīngqílín

idea (n.) 想法, 主意 xiǎngfǎ, zhǔyì

if (conj.) 如果 rúguǒ

ill (adj.) 有病的 yǒubìngde

immediately (adv.) 立刻 lìkè

import (n., v.) 进口 jìnkǒu

important (adj.) 重要的 zhòngyàode

impossible (adj.) 不可能的 bùkěnéngde

improve (v.) 改善 gǎishàn

in (prep.) 在…里 zài…lǐ

in order to (id.) 为了… wèile…

include (v.) 包括 bāokuò

income (n.) 收入 shōurù

inconvenient (adj.) 不便的 bùbiànde

increase (v.) 增加 zēngjiā

independence (n.) 独立 dúlì

indoors (adv.) 户内 hùnèi

industrial (adj.) 工业的 gōngyède

inexpensive (adj.) 便宜的 piányide

information (n.) 消息, 信息 xiāoxi, xìnxī

injured (adj.) 受伤的 shòushāngde

inside (adv.) 在里面 zài lǐmiàn

instruction(s) (n.) 说明, 说明书 shuōmíng, shuōmíngshū

instrument (musical) (n.) 乐器 yuèqì

intelligent (adj.) 聪明的 cōngmingde

intend to (v.) 打算 dǎsuan

interesting (adj.) 有趣的 yǒuqùde

intermediate (level) (adj.) 中级的 zhōngjíde

international (adj.) 国际 guójì

interpret (v.) 口译 kǒuyì

interpreter (n.) 口译员 kǒuyìyuán

intersection (n.) 十字路口 shízìlùkǒu

interview (n., v.) 面谈; 采访 miàntán; cǎifǎng

into (prep.) 进入 jìnrù

introduce (v.) 介绍 jièshào

invest (v.) 投资 tóuzī

invite (v.) 邀请 yāoqǐng

island (n.) 岛 dǎo

issue (magazine) (n.) 期 qī

J

jacket (n.) 上衣 shàngyī

January (n.) 一月 yīyuè

jeep (n.) 吉普车 jípǔchē

job (n.) 工作 gōngzuò

jog (v.) 慢跑 mànpǎo

joke (v., n.) 开玩笑; 玩笑 kāi wánxiào; wánxiào

juice (n.) 果汁 guǒzhī

July (n.) 七月 qīyuè

June (n.) 六月 liùyuè

jungle (n.) 丛林 cónglín

just (quite recently) (adv.) 刚刚 gānggāng

K

keep (v.) 保持 bǎochí

key (n.) 钥匙 yàoshi

kilogram (n.) 公斤 gōngjīn

kilometer (n.) 公里 gōnglǐ

kind (adj., n.) 和蔼的, 善良的; 种类 héǎide, shànliángde; zhǒnglèi

kitchen (n.) 厨房 chúfáng

kite (n.) 风筝 fēngzheng

knife (n.) 刀 dāo

knock (v.) 敲 qiāo

know (v.) 知道 zhīdào

know (get to know) (v.) 结识, 发现 jiéshí, fāxiàn

L

labor (n., v.) 劳动 láodòng

lacquer (n.) 漆 qī

lake (n.) 湖 hú

land (n.) 陆地, 土地 lùdì, tǔdì

land (an airplane) (v.) 着陆 zhuólù

landlord (n.) 房东 fángdōng

language (n.) 语言 yǔyán

lantern (n.) 灯, 灯笼 dēng, dēnglong

large (adj.) 大的 dàde

last month (adv.) 上个月 shàng ge yuè

last night (adv.) 昨晚 zuówǎn

last week (adv.) 上周 shàngzhōu

late (adj.) 迟的, 晚的 chíde, wǎnde

later (adv.) 后来 hòulái

laugh (v.) 笑 xiào

laundry room (n.) 洗衣房 xǐyīfáng

lavatory (n.) 盥洗室 guànxǐshì

law (n.) 法律 fǎlù

lazy (adj.) 懒惰的 lǎnduòde

lead (v.) 领导 lǐngdǎo

leaf (n.) 树叶 shùyè

learn (v.) 学习 xuéxí

least (at least) (adj.) 最小的, 最少的
    zuìxiǎode, zuìshǎode

leave (depart from a place) (v.) 离开 líkāi

leave a message (id.) 留言 liúyán

left (turn left) (n.) 左边 zuǒbian

lemonade (n.) 柠檬汁 níngméngzhī

length (n.) 长度 chángdù

lesson (n.) 课 kè

let (v.) 让 ràng

letter (to a friend) (n.) 信 xìn

library (n.) 图书馆 túshūguǎn

license (n.) 执照 zhízhào

lie down (v.) 躺下 tǎng xià

life (n.) 生命, 生活 shēngmìng, shēnghuó

life jacket (n.) 救生衣 jiùshēngyī

lift (v.) 举起 jǔqǐ

light (n.) 光, 灯 guāng, dēng

light (adj.) 轻的 qīngde

like (prep.) 象 xiàng

like (v.) 喜欢 xǐhuan

line (n.) 线, 队 xiàn, duì

listen (v.) 听 tīng

liter (n.) 公升 gōngshēng

literature (n.) 文学 wénxué

litter (v.) 乱丢 luàndiū

little (adj.) 少的, 小的 shǎode, xiǎode

live (v.) 住 zhù

livingroom (n.) 客厅 kètīng

local (adj.) 当地的 dāngdìde

lock (n., v.) 锁住; 锁 suǒzhù; suǒ

long (adj.) 长的 chángde

look (appear) (v.) 显得 xiǎnde

look at (v.) 看 kàn

look for (v.) 找 zhǎo

lose (sth.) (v.) 丢 diū

lose one's way (id.) 迷路 mílù

lose weight (id.) 体重减轻 tǐzhòng jiǎnqīng

loud(ly) (adj., adv.) 大声的; 大声地 dàshēngde; dàshēngde

love (n., v.) 爱 ài

lucky (adj.) 幸运的 xìngyùnde

luggage (n.) 行李 xíngli

lunch (n.) 午饭 wǔfàn

M

machine (n.) 机器 jīqì

magazine (n.) 杂志 zázhì

mail (n., v.) 邮件; 邮寄 yóujiàn; yóujì

major (field of knowledge) (n.) 主修, 专业 zhǔxiū, zhuānyè

major in (v.) 主修 zhǔxiū

majority (n.) 大多数 dàduōshù

make (v.) 制造, 做 zhìzào, zuò

male (adj.) 男的 nánde

man (n.) 男人 nánrén

manage (v.) 管理 guǎnlǐ

management (n.) 管理 guǎnlǐ

manager (n.) 经理 jīnglǐ

manufacture (v.) 制造 zhìzào

many (adj.) 许多的 xǔduōde

map (n.) 地图 dìtú

marble (n.) 大理石 dàlǐshí

March (n.) 三月 sānyuè

market (n.) 市场 shìchǎng

married (adj.) 已婚的 yǐhūnde

mat (sleeping mat) (n.) 席子 xízi

matches (n.) 火柴 huǒchái

material/fabric (n.) 布料 bùliào

mattress (n.) 席梦思 xímèngsī

may (aux.) 可能, 可以 kěnéng, kěyǐ

May (n.) 五月 wǔyuè

maybe (adv.) 也许 yěxǔ

me (pron.) 我 wǒ

meal (n.) 餐, 饭 cān, fàn

means (of transportation) (n.) 交通工具
    jiāotōng gōngjù

measure (v.) 测量 cèliáng

measurement (n.) 度量 dùliàng

meat (n.) 肉 ròu

mechanic (n.) 技工, 修理工 jìgōng, xiūlǐgōng

meet (v.) 遇见, 开会 yùjiàn, kāihuì

meet (in order to pick up) (v.) 接 jiē

meeting (n.) 会议 huìyì

member (n.) 成员 chéngyuán

mend (v.) 改进, 修 gǎijìn, xiū

menu (n.) 菜单 càidān

message (n.) 信息, 留言 xìnxī, liúyán

meter (n.) 公尺, 米 gōngchǐ, mǐ

meticulous (adj.) 一丝不苟的 yīsībùgǒude

middle (n.) 中间 zhōngjiān

midnight (n.) 午夜 wǔyè

military (n., adj.) 军队; 军事的 jūnduì;
　　jūnshìde

milk (n.) 牛奶 niúnǎi

million (n.) 百万 bǎiwàn

minimum (n.) 最少数 zuìshǎoshù

ministry (government) (n.) 部 bù

minority (n.) 少数, 少数民族 shǎoshù,
　　shǎoshù mínzú

minute (n.) 分钟 fēnzhōng

mirror (n.) 镜子 jìngzi

Miss (hon.) 小姐 Xiǎojie

miss (v.) 思念, 错过 sī'niàn, cuòguò

missionary (n.) 传教士 chuánjiàoshì

mistake (n.) 错误 cuòwù

misunderstand (v.) 误会 wùhuì

mix (v.) 混合, 混淆 hùnhé, hùnxiáo

modern (adj.) 现代的 xiàndàide

moment (n.) 时刻 shíkè

money (n.) 钱 qián

monk (n.) 和尚 héshang

month (n.) 月 yuè

monthly (adj.) 每月一次的 měi yuè yī cì de

moon (n.) 月亮 yuèliang

more (adj.) 更多的 gèng duō de

more than (exp.) 多于 duōyú

morning (n.) 早上, 上午 zǎoshang, shàngwǔ

mosquito (n.) 蚊子 wénzi

mother (n.) 母亲, 妈妈 mǔqīn, māma

mother-in-law (n.) 岳母, 婆婆 yuèmǔ, pópo

motorbike/motorcycle (n.) 摩托车 mótuōchē

mountain (n.) 山 shān

mouth (n.) 嘴 zuǐ

move (into a new home) (v.) 搬 bān

movie (n.) 电影 diànyǐng

movie theater (n.) 电影院 diànyǐngyuàn

Mr. (hon.) 先生 Xiānsheng

Mrs. (hon.) 太太 Tàitai

much (adj., adv.) 许多; 大量地 xǔduō; dàliàngde

muddy (adj.) 泥泞的 ní'nìngde

museum (n.) 博物馆 bówùguǎn

music (n.) 音乐 yīnyuè

musical instrument (n.) 乐器 yuèqì

musician (n.) 音乐家 yīnyuèjiā

Muslim (n.) 穆斯林 Mùsīlín

must (aux.) 必须 bìxū

my (pron.) 我的 wǒde

N

name (n.) 名字 míngzi

napkin (n.) 餐巾纸 cānjīnzhǐ

narrow (adj.) 狭窄的 xiázhǎide

nation (n.) 国家 guójiā

national (adj.) 国家的, 全国的 guójiāde, quánguóde

nationality (n.) 国籍 guójí

native (adj.) 土生的, 本族的 tǔshēngde, běnzúde

natural (adj.) 自然的 zìránde

nature (n.) 自然 zìrán

navy (military) (n.) 海军 hǎijūn

near (adj.) 近 jìn

neat (tidy) (adj.) 整洁的 zhěngjiéde

necessary (adj.) 必要的 bìyàode

necklace (n.) 项链 xiàngliàn

need (n., v.) 需要 xūyào

needle (n.) 针 zhēn

neighborhood (n.) 街道 jiēdào

nephew (n.) 侄子, 外甥 zhízi, wàisheng

nervous (adj.) 紧张的 jǐnzhāngde

never (adv.) 从不 cóngbù

never (yet) (adv.) 尚未 shàngwèi

never mind (id.) 算了 suàn le

new (adj.) 新的 xīnde

news (n.) 新闻 xīnwén

newspaper (n.) 报纸 bàozhǐ

next (adj.) 下一, 紧邻的 xiàyī, jǐnlínde

next to (prep.) 在…旁边 zài...pángbiān

next week (n., adv.) 下星期 xià xīngqī

nice (adj.) 好的 hǎode

niece (n.) 侄女, 外甥女 zhí'nǚ, wàishengnǚ

night (n.) 夜里 yèli

no (adv.) 不 bù

no more (exp.) 不再 búzài

nobody (pron.) 无人 wúrén

noisy (adj.) 嘈杂的 cāozáde

nongovernmental organization (NGO) (n.) 非
  政府组织 fēizhèngfǔ zǔzhī

noodle soup (n.) 汤面 tāngmiàn

noon (n.) 中午 zhōngwǔ

normal (adj.) 正常的 zhèngchángde

north (n.) 北方, 北部 běifāng,běibù

northern (adj.) 北方的 běifāngde

northerner (n.) 北方人 běifāngrén

nose (n.) 鼻子 bízi

not yet (exp.) 尚未 shàngwèi

notebook (n.) 笔记本 bǐjiběn

nothing (pron.) 没有东西 méi yǒu dōngxi

novel (n.) 小说 xiǎoshuō

November (n.) 十一月 shíyīyuè

now (adv.) 现在 xiànzài

nowadays (adv.) 现今 xiànjīn

nowhere (adv.) 无处 wúchù

number (n.) 数字 shùzì

nurse (n.) 护士 hùshi

O

occasion (n.) 场合 chǎnghé

occasionally (adv.) 偶尔 ǒu'ěr

ocean (n.) 海洋 hǎiyáng

o'clock (adv.) 点 diǎn

October (n.) 十月 shíyuè

of (belonging to) (prep.) 的 de

offer (v.) 提供 tígòng

office (n.) 办公室 bàngōngshì

official (n., adj.) 官员; 官方的 guānyuán; guānfāngde

often (adv.) 常常 chángcháng

oh (interj.) 啊 ā

oil (n.) 油 yóu

okay (interj.) 好, 行, 好吧 hǎo, xíng, hǎoba

old (describing people) (adj.) 老的 lǎode

old (describing things) (adj.) 旧的 jiùde

older than (exp.) 比...大 bǐ...dà

old-fashioned (adj.) 老式的 lǎoshìde

on (prep.) 在...上 zài...shàng

on time (id.) 准时 zhǔnshí

one (two, three...) (n.) 一 yī

only (adv.) 只 zhǐ

open (v.,adj.) 开, 打开; 开着 kāi, dǎkāi; kāizhe

opera (n.) 歌剧 gējù

operation (surgery) (n.) 手术 shǒushù

opinion (n.) 意见 yìjiàn

opinion (in my opinion) (id.) 依我看来 yī wǒ kàn lái

opportunity (n.) 机会 jīhuì

opposite (facing) (prep.) 在...对面 zài...duìmiàn

or (conj.) 或者 huòzhě

orange (color) (n.) 橙色 chéngsè

orange (fruit) (n.) 桔子 júzi

orange juice (n.) 橙汁 chéngzhī

order (food and/or drink) (v.) 点 diǎn

order (sb. to do sth.) (v.) 命令 mìnglìng

ordinary (adj.) 平常的, 普通的 píngchángde, pǔtōngde

organization (n.) 组织 zǔzhī

other (adj.) 别的 biéde

ought to (aux.) 应该 yīnggāi

out (adv.) 向外, 出 xiàngwài, chū

outdoors (adv.) 户外 hùwài

outside (adv., prep.) 外面; 在...外面 wàimian; zài...wàimian

over (prep.) 在...上 zài...shàng

over there (id.) 在那边 zài nà biān

overnight (adv.) 一夜之间 yī yè zhī jiān

overseas (adv., adj.) 在海外; 海外的 zài hǎiwài; hǎiwàide

owe (v.) 欠 qiàn

own (v., adj.) 拥有; 自己的 yōngyǒu; zìjǐde

P

pack (n., v.) 一包; 打包 yī bāo; dǎbāo

package/parcel (n.) 包裹 bāoguǒ

paddy (n.) 稻谷 dàogǔ

page (n.) 页 yè

pagoda (n.) 宝塔 bǎotǎ

painful (sore) (adj.) 疼痛的 téngtòngde

painter (artist) (n.) 画家 huàjiā

painting/picture (n.) 画 huà

pair (n.) 一对, 一双, 一副 yí duì, yì shuāng, yí fù

pants (n.) 裤子 kùzi

paper (piece of paper) (n.) 纸 zhǐ

parents (n.) 父母 fùmǔ

park (n.) 公园 gōngyuán

park (v.) 停车 tíngchē

parking lot (n.) 停车场 tíngchēchǎng

part (n.) 部分 bùfen

participate (v.) 参加 cānjiā

partner (n.) 合伙人, 合作伙伴 héhuǒrén, hézuò huǒbàn

part-time (adj.) 半职的 bànzhíde

party (n.) 社交聚会 shèjiāo jùhuì

pass (v.) 通过 tōngguò

passenger (n.) 乘客 chéngkè

passport (n.) 护照 hùzhào

past (n.) 过去 guòqù

pay (v., n.) 支付; 工资 zhīfù; gōngzī

peace (n.) 和平 hépíng

peaceful (adj.) 和平的 hépíngde

peasant (n.) 农民 nóngmín

peel (v.) 剥, 削 bō, xuē

pen (n.) 钢笔 gāngbǐ

performance (n.) 表演 biǎoyǎn

perhaps (adv.) 也许 yěxǔ

permission (n.) 许可, 允许 xǔkě, yǔnxǔ

permit (n.) 许可证 xǔkězhèng

person (n.) 人 rén

Ph.D. (n.) 博士 bóshì

phone (n.) 电话 diànhuà

photograph/picture (n.) 照片 zhàopiàn

pickpocket (n.) 扒手 páshǒu

piece (n.) 片, 块, 张, 个 piàn, kuài, zhāng, gè

picture (take a picture) (id.) 拍照 pāizhào

pill (n.) 药丸 yàowán

pillow (n.) 枕头 zhěntou

pillowcase (n.) 枕头套 zhěntoutào

pilot (n.) 飞行员 fēixíngyuán

pink (adj.) 粉红色的 fěnhóngsède

place (n.) 地方 dìfāng

place (v.) 置, 放 zhì, fàng

plain/simple (adj.) 简单的 jiǎndānde

plan (n., v.) 计划 jìhuà

plane (n.) 飞机 fēijī

plant (rice) (v.) 种 zhòng

plate (n.) 盘子 pánzi

platform (railway) (n.) 月台 yuètái

play (v.) 玩 wán

pleasant (adj.) 愉快的 yúkuàide

please (polite) (v.) 请 qǐng

poetry (n.) 诗 shī

police officer (n.) 警察 jǐngchá

policy (n.) 政策 zhèngcè

polite (adj.) 有礼貌的 yǒulǐmàode

politics (n.) 政治 zhèngzhì

pond (n.) 池塘 chítáng

pool (swimming pool) (n.) 游泳池 yóuyǒngchí

poor (adj.) 穷的 qióngde

popular (adj.) 流行的, 受欢迎的 liúxíngde, shòu huānyíng de

population (n.) 人口 rénkǒu

pork (n.) 猪肉 zhūròu

port (n.) 港口 gǎngkǒu

possible (adj.) 可能的 kěnéngde

possibly (adv.) 可能地 kěnéngde

post office (n.) 邮局 yóujú

postage (n.) 邮资 yóuzī

postcard (n.) 明信片 míngxìnpiàn

pottery (n.) 陶器 táoqì

pour (v.) 倒 (水) dào (shuǐ)

poverty (n.) 贫困 pínkùn

powerful (adj.) 强大的 qiángdàde

practical (adj.) 实用的 shíyòngde

practice (v.) 实践, 练习 shíjiàn, liànxí

pray (v.) 祈求, 祷告 qíqiú, dǎogào

prefer (v.) 偏爱 piān'ài

pregnant (adj.) 怀孕的 huáiyùnde

prescription (n.) 处方 chǔfāng

present/gift (n.) 礼物 lǐwù

president (of a country) (n.) 总统 zǒngtǒng

pretty (adj., adv.) 漂亮的; 非常 piàoliangde; fēicháng

price (n.) 价格 jiàgé

priest (n.) 牧师 mùshī

print (v.) 印刷 yìnshuā

printer (machine) (n.) 打印机 dǎyìnjī

private (adj.) 私人的 sīrénde

probably (adv.) 很可能地 hěn kěnéng de

problem (n.) 难题, 问题, 麻烦 nántí, wèntí, máfan

produce (v.) 生产 shēngchǎn

professor (n.) 教授 jiàoshòu

profit (n.) 利润 lìrùn

program (n.) 节目, 计划, 项目 jiémù, jìhuà, xiàngmù

promise (n., v.) 允诺 yǔnnuò

pronounce (v.) 发音 fāyīn

pronunciation (n.) 发音 fāyīn

proposal (n.) 建议 jiànyì

proverb (n.) 谚语 yànyǔ

province (n.) 省 shěng

public (adj.) 公开的, 对外的 gōngkāide, duìwàide

public (n.) 公众, 公立 gōngzhòng, gōnglì

publish (v.) 出版, 发表 chūbǎn, fābiǎo

purse (n.) 钱包 qiánbāo

push (v.) 推 tuī

Q

quality (n.) 质量 zhìliàng

question (n.) 问题 wèntí

queue (line) (n.) 队 duì

quick(ly) (adj., adv.) 迅速的; 迅速地 xùnsùde; xùnsùde

quiet (adj.) 安静的 ānjìngde

R

radio (n.) 收音机 shōuyīnjī

rain (n., v.) 雨; 下雨 yǔ; xiàyǔ

raincoat (n.) 雨衣 yǔyī

rat (n.) 老鼠 lǎoshǔ

rate of exchange (n.) 兑换率 duìhuànlǜ

raw (adj.) 生的 shēngde

razor (n.) 刀片 dāopiàn

read (v.) 读, 看书 dú, kànshū

ready (willing) (adj.) 乐意的 lèyìde

real (adj.) 真实的 zhēnshíde

really? (exp.) 真的吗? zhēndema?

reason (n.) 理由 lǐyóu

receipt (n.) 收据 shōujù

receive (sth.) (v.) 收到 shōudào

receptionist (n.) 接待员 jiēdàiyuán

recipe (n.) 菜谱 càipǔ

recommend (v.) 推荐 tuījiàn

recover (from illness) (v.) 痊愈 quányù

red (adj.) 红色的 hóngsède

refrigerator (n.) 冰箱 bīngxiāng

refugee (n.) 难民 nànmín

region (n.) 地区 dìqū

regularly (adv.) 有规律地, 定期地
　　yǒuguīlùde, dìngqīde

relationship (n.) 关系 guānxì

relative(s) (n.) 亲戚 qīnqì

relax (v.) 放松 fàngsōng

religion (n.) 宗教 zōngjiào

remember (v.) 记得 jide

rent (v.) 租 zū

rent (money) (n.) 租金 zūjīn

repair (v.) 修理 xiūlǐ

repeat (v.) 重复 chóngfù

reply (n., v.) 答复 dáfù

report (n., v.) 报告 bàogào

reporter (n.) 记者 jìzhě

representative (n.) 代表 dàibiǎo

research (v.) 研究 yánjiū

researcher (n.) 研究员 yánjiūyuán

resemble (v.) 象 xiàng

reserve/make a reservation (v.) 预订 yùdìng

resort (place) (n.) 度假胜地 dùjià shèngdi

respect (n., v.) 尊敬 zūnjìng

responsibility (n.) 责任 zérèn

rest (n., v.) 休息 xiūxi

restaurant (n.) 餐馆 cānguǎn

restroom (n.) 厕所 cèsuǒ

resume/CV (n.) 简历, 学历 jiǎnlì, xuélì

retire (from working) (v.) 退休 tuìxiū

return (go home) (v.) 回 huí

return (sth.) (v.) 归还 guīhuán

review (v.) 复习, 审阅 fùxí, shěnyuè

rice (cooked) (n.) 米饭 mǐfàn

rice (raw) (n.) 米 mǐ

rice bowl (n.) 饭碗 fànwǎn

rice cake (n.) 米糕 mǐgāo

rice paddy (n.) 稻田 dàotián

rice wine (n.) 米酒 mǐjiǔ

rich (wealthy) (adj.) 有钱的 yǒuqiánde

ride (a bike) (v.) 骑 qí

right (correct) (adj.) 正确的 zhèngquède

right (turn right) (n.) 右边 yòubian

right now (id.) 现在, 马上 xiànzài, mǎshàng

ring (n.) 环, 戒指 huán, jièzhi

rinse (one's mouth) (v.) 漱口 shùkǒu

river (n.) 河 hé

road (n.) 路 lù

rob (v.) 抢劫 qiǎngjié

romantic (adj.) 浪漫的 làngmànde

room (n.) 房间 fángjiān

rose (n.) 玫瑰 méigui

row(ofseats) (n.) 排 pái

run (v.) 跑 pǎo

run into sth./sb. (v.) 遇见 yùjiàn

rush (n., v.) 急; 匆忙 jí; cōngmáng

S

sad (adj.) 悲伤的 bēishāngde

safe (adj.) 安全的 ānquánde

salad (n.) 沙拉 shālā

salary (n.) 工资 gōngzī

salt (n.) 盐 yán

salty (adj.) 咸的 xiánde

same (adj.) 相同的 xiāngtóngde

sample (n.) 样品 yàngpǐn

sandal (n.) 凉鞋 liángxié

save (money) (v.) 存 cún

say (v.) 说 shuō

scarf (n.) 围巾 wéijīn

scenic spot (n.) 风景点 fēngjǐngdiǎn

schedule an appointment (id.) 约时间 yuē shíjiān

scholarship (n.) 奖学金 jiǎngxuéjīn

school (n.) 学校 xuéxiào

science (n.) 科学 kēxué

scientist (n.) 科学家 kēxuéjiā

scissors (n.) 剪刀 jiǎndāo

sea (n.) 海 hǎi

season (n.) 季节 jìjié

seat (n.) 座位 zuòwèi

second (in rank or order) (adj.) 第二 dì'èr

second-class (adj.) 二等 èrděng

secretary (n.) 秘书 mìshū

see (v.) 看见 kànjiàn

seem (v.) 好像 hǎoxiàng

sentence (of words) (n.) 句子 jùzi

separate(ly) (adj., adv.) 分开地 fēnkāide

September (n.) 九月 Jiǔyuè

serious (adj.) 严肃的, 认真的 yánsùde, rènzhēnde

service (n.) 服务 fúwù

set the table (id.) 摆餐具 bǎi cānjù

several (adj.) 几（个） jǐ(ge)

sew (v.) 缝 féng

shake hands with (id.) 与...握手 yǔ...wòshǒu

shampoo (n.) 洗发液 xǐfāyè

share (v.) 共有, 共用 gòngyǒu, gòngyòng

shave (v.) 剃, 刮 tì, guā

she (pron.) 她 tā

sheet (bed) (n.) 被单 bèidān

sheet (paper) (n.) 纸张 zhǐzhāng

ship (n.) 船 chuán

shirt (n.) 衬衫 chènshān

shoe (n.) 鞋子 xiézi

shop (n.) 商店 shāngdiàn

shop (v.) 购物 gòuwù

short (in height) (adj.) 矮 ǎi

short (in length) (adj.) 短 duǎn

shortage (n.) 短缺 duǎnquē

shorten (v.) 缩短 suōduǎn

shorts (n.) 短裤 duǎnkù

should (aux.) 应该 yīnggāi

show (express) (v.) 表示 biǎoshì

show sb. around (id.) 领人参观 lǐngrén cānguān

shower (n.) 淋浴 línyù

shower (take a shower) (id.) 洗澡 xǐzǎo

shrimp (n.) 虾 xiā

shy (adj.) 腼腆的 miǎntiǎnde

sick (adj.) 有病的 yǒubìngde

side (left or right) (n.) 边 biān

sightsee (v.) 观光 guānguāng

sightseer (n.) 观光客 guānguāngkè

sign (v.) 签名 qiānmíng

signature (n.) 签名 qiānmíng

silk (n.) 丝绸 sīchóu

silver (n.) 银 yín

simple (adj.) 简单的 jiǎndānde

since (conj.) 自...以来 zì...yǐlái

sincere (adj.) 真诚的 zhēnchéngde

sincerely yours (id.) 此致...敬礼 cǐzhì...jìnglǐ

sing (v.) 唱 chàng

singer (n.) 歌手 gēshǒu

single (unmarried) (adj.) 单身的 dānshēnde

sister (older) (n.) 姐姐 jiějie

sister (younger) (n.) 妹妹 mèimei

sister-in-law (n.) 嫂子, 姑子, 弟媳, 姨子 sǎozi, gūzǐ, dìxí, yízi

sit (v.) 坐 zuò

situation (n.) 情形, 情况 qíngxing, qíngkuàng

size (n.) 尺寸 chǐcùn

skilled (adj.) 熟练的 shúliànde

skirt (n.) 短裙 duǎnqún

sky (n.) 天空 tiānkōng

slang (n.) 俚语 lǐyǔ

sleep (v.) 睡 shuì

sleeping bag (n.) 睡袋 shuìdài

sleepy (adj.) 困 kùn

sleeve (n.) 袖子 xiùzi

slice (n.) 一片 yípiàn

slipper(s) (n.) 拖鞋 tuōxié

slippery (adj.) 滑的 huáde

slow down (v.) 慢下来 màn xiàlái

slow(ly) (adj., adv.) 缓慢的; 缓慢地 huǎnmànde; huǎnmànde

small (adj.) 小的 xiǎode

smart (adj.) 聪明的 cōngmingde

smell (v.) 闻 wén

smile (n., v.) 微笑 wēixiào

smoke (v., n.) 抽烟; 烟 chōuyān; yān

snow (n., v.) 雪; 下雪 xuě; xiàxuě

so (+adj) (adv.) 如此 rú cǐ

soap (n.) 肥皂 féizào

social worker (n.) 社会工作者 shèhuì gōngzuòzhě

society (n.) 社会 shèhuì

sock (n.) 短袜 duǎnwà

soda (n.) 苏打 sūdá

soda water (n.) 苏打水 sūdáshuǐ

soft (adj.) 软的 ruǎnde

soldier (n.) 士兵 shìbīng

sold-out (adj.) 已售完 yǐ shòu wán

sometimes (adv.) 有时 yǒushí

son (n.) 儿子 érzi

song (n.) 歌 gē

son-in-law (n.) 女婿 nǚxù

soon (as soon as possible) (adv.) 不久, 很快 bùjiǔ, hěnkuài

sorry (adj.) 抱歉, 对不起 bàoqiàn, duìbuqǐ

sound (n.) 声音 shēngyīn

soup (n.) 汤 tāng

sour (adj.) 酸的 suānde

south (n.) 南方, 南部 nánfāng, nánbù

southern (adj.) 南方的 nánfāngde

southerner (n.) 南方人 nánfāngrén

souvenir (n.) 纪念品 jìniànpǐn

speak (v.) 说 shuō

special (adj.) 特别的 tèbiéde

specialize in (v.) 擅长于 shàncháng yú

speed limit (n.) 速度极限 sùdù jíxiàn

speed up (v.) 加速 jiāsù

spell (v.) 拼写 pīnxiě

spoon (n.) 汤匙 tāngchí

sport (n.) 运动 yùndòng

spring (season) (n.) 春天 chūntiān

stadium (n.) 体育场 tǐyùchǎng

staff (n.) 员工 yuángōng

stair(s) (n.) 楼梯 lóutī

stamp (n.) 邮票 yóupiào

stand (v.) 站 zhàn

standard of living (id.) 生活水平 shēnghuó shuǐpíng

star (n.) 星 xīng

start (n., v.) 开始 kāishǐ

state (of the fifty states) (n.) 州 zhōu

statue (n.) 雕像 diāoxiàng

stay (v., n.) 住; 停留 zhù; tíngliú

stay up (v.) 熬夜 áoyè

steal (v.) 偷 tōu

sticky (adj.) 粘的 niánde

still (adv.) 仍然, 还 réngrán, hái

stop (v.) 停 tíng

store (n.) 商店 shāngdiàn

storm (n.) 风暴 fēngbào

story (n.) 故事 gùshi

straight (adv.) 一直 yìzhí

street (n.) 街 jiē

street vendor (n.) 街头小贩 jiētóu xiǎofàn

strength (n.) 力量 lìliàng

string (n.) 串，线 chuàn, xiàn

strong (adj.) 强壮的, 强大的 qiángzhuàngde, qiángdàde

student (n.) 学生 xuésheng

study (n., v.) 学习 xuéxí

study abroad (v.) 留学 liúxué

subject (school subject) (n.) 课程 kèchéng

submit an application (id.) 递交申请 dìjiāo shēnqǐng

subscribe to (v.) 订 dìng

suburb(s) (n.) 郊区 jiāoqū

subway (n.) 地铁 dìtiě

successful (adj.) 成功的 chénggōngde

such as (id.) 例如 lìrú

suddenly (adv.) 突然 tūrán

sugar (n.) 糖 táng

suit (n.) 套装, 西装 tàozhuāng, xīzhuāng

suitcase (n.) 手提箱 shǒutíxiāng

summer (n.) 夏天 xiàtiān

sun (n.) 太阳 tàiyáng

sunglasses (n.) 太阳镜 tàiyángjìng

sunny (adj.) 晴朗的 qínglǎngde

sunrise (n.) 日出 rìchū

sunset (n.) 日落 rìluò

supermarket (n.) 超市 chāoshì

support (one's family) (v.) 养家 yǎngjiā

surely/certainly (adv.) 的确, 一定, 当然 díquè, yídìng, dāngrán

surname (last name) (n.) 姓 xìng

surprise (n.) 惊奇 jīngqí

sweat (n.) 汗 hàn

sweaty (adj.) 汗湿的 hànshīde

sweet (adj.) 甜的 tiánde

swim (v.) 游泳 yóuyǒng

swimming pool (n.) 游泳池 yóuyǒngchí

swimming trunks (n.) 泳裤 yǒngkù

swimsuit (n.) 泳衣 yǒngyī

T

table (n.) 桌子 zhuōzi

tailor (n.) 裁缝 cáifeng

take (v.) 拿 ná

take off (clothes) (v.) 脱掉 tuōdiào

take off (plane) (v.) 起飞 qǐfēi

take-out/take-away (food) (adj.) 外卖, 拿走吃 wàimài, ná zǒu chī

talk (n., v.) 谈; 讲话 tán; jiǎnghuà

tall (adj.) 高的 gāode

tape (adhesive tape) (n.) 胶带 jiāodài

tape measure (n.) 卷尺 juǎnchǐ

tape recorder (n.) 录音机 lùyīnjī

taste (n., v.) 尝; 味道 cháng; wèidao

tax (n.) 税 shuì

taxi (n.) 出租车 chūzūchē

tea (n.) 茶 chá

teach (v.) 教 jiāo

teacher (n.) 老师 lǎoshī

team (n.) 队 duì

telephone (n.) 电话 diànhuà

telephone directory (n.) 电话簿 diànhuàbù

television (n.) 电视 diànshì

tell (v.) 告诉 gàosu

temperature (n.) 温度 wēndù

temple (n.) 庙 miào

temporary (adj.) 暂时的, 临时的 zànshíde, línshíde

ten (n.) 十 shí

tennis (n.) 网球 wǎngqiú

tent (n.) 帐篷 zhàngpeng

terrorism (n.) 恐怖主义 kǒngbùzhǔyì

textbook (n.) 教科书, 教材 jiàokēshū, jiàocái

thank (thank you) (v.) 谢谢 xièxie

thanks to (id.) 由于, 因为 yóuyú, yīnwèi

that (pron.) 那 nà

their (pron.) 他们的 tāmende

them (pron.) 他们 tāmen

then (adv.) 然后 ránhòu

there (adv.) 在那里 zài nàli

there is/are (id.) 有, 存在 yǒu, cúnzài

therefore (adv.) 因此, 所以 yīncǐ, suǒyǐ

they (pron.) 他们 tāmen

thin (describing people) (adj.) 瘦的 shòude

thing (n.) 事, 物, 东西 shì,wù,dōngxi

think (v.) 想, 认为 xiǎng, rènwéi

thirsty (adj.) 口渴的 kǒukěde

this (pron.) 这 zhè

thousand (n.) 千 qiān

thread (n.) 线 xiàn

throughout (prep.) 遍及, 四处 biànjí, sìchù

ticket (n.) 票 piào

tie (v.) 系 xì

tie (n.) 领带 lǐngdài

tight (adj.) 紧的 jǐndi

time (n.) 时间 shíjiān

tip (gratuity) (n.) 小费 xiǎofèi

tired (adj.) 疲倦的 píjuànde

tissue (n.) 擦手纸 cāshǒuzhǐ

to (prep.) 向, 到, 对 xiàng, dào, duì

toast (v.) 祝酒, 烤 zhùjiǔ, kǎo

today (adv., n.) 今天 jīntiān

together (adv.) 一起 yìqǐ

toilet (n.) 厕所 cèsuǒ

toilet paper (n.) 卫生纸 wèishēngzhǐ

tomato (n.) 西红柿 xīhóngshì

tomorrow (adv., n.) 明天 míngtiān

ton (n.) 吨 dūn

tonight (adv., n.) 今夜, 今晚 jīnyè, jīnwǎn

too much/many (exp.) 太多 tài duō

tooth (n.) 牙齿 yáchǐ

total (n.) 总数 zǒngshù

tour guide (n.) 导游 dǎoyóu

tourist (n.) 游客 yóukè

towel (n.) 毛巾 máojīn

town (n.) 城镇 chéngzhèn

trade (n.) 贸易 màoyì

tradition (n.) 传统 chuántǒng

traditional (adj.) 传统的 chuántǒngde

traffic (n.) 交通 jiāotōng

traffic jam (n.) 交通堵塞 jiāotōng dǔsè

traffic light (n.) 红绿灯 hónglùdēng

trail (n.) 小道 xiǎodào

train (n.) 火车 huǒchē

train (v.) 训练 xùnliàn

194

train station (n.) 火车站 huǒchēzhàn

transfer (money) (v.) 转帐 zhuǎnzhàng

translate (v.) 翻译 fānyì

translation (work) (n.) 翻译 fānyì

translator (person) (n.) 翻译 fānyì

travel (v.) 旅行 lǚxíng

traveler's check(s) (n.) 旅行支票 lǚxíng zhīpiào

tray (n.) 托盘 tuōpán

treat (sb. to meal) (v.) 请客 qǐngkè

tree (n.) 树 shù

trip (n.) 旅行 lǚxíng

tropics (n.) 热带 rèdài

truck (n.) 卡车 kǎchē

true (adj.) 真实的 zhēnshíde

trust (n., v.) 信任 xìnrèn

try (some food) (v.) 尝 cháng

try (sth.on, to do sth.) (v.) 试 shì

T-shirt (n.) T 恤衫 T-xùshān

tuition (n.) 学费 xuéfèi

turn (v.) 转弯 zhuǎnwān

turn off (a lamp/lights) (v.) 关 guān

turn on (a lamp/lights) (v.) 开 kāi

U

ugly (adj.) 丑陋的 chǒulòude

umbrella (n.) 伞 sǎn

unable to (adj.) 不能 bù néng

uncle (n.) 叔叔, 伯伯, 舅舅 shūshu, bóbo, jiùjiu

uncomfortable (adj.) 不舒服的 bùshūfude

under (prep.) 在…之下 zài…zhīxià

underclothes (n.) 内衣 nèiyī

underground (adj.) 地下的 dìxiàde

understand (v.) 懂, 理解 dǒng, lǐjiě

unemployed (adj.) 失业的 shīyède

unfortunate (adj.) 不幸的 búxìngde

uniform (n.) 制服 zhìfú

unique (adj.) 独特的 dútède

university (n.) 大学 dàxué

unless (conj.) 除非 chúfēi

unload (v.) 卸货 xièhuò

unpack (luggage) (v.) 开包 kāi bāo

unusual (adj.) 不寻常的 bù xúncháng de

up (adv.) 上 shàng

upstairs (adv.) 在楼上 zài lóushàng

urgent (adj.) 紧急的 jǐnjíde

use (n., v.) 用处; 使用 yòngchù; shǐyòng

used (adj.) 旧的, 二手的 jiùde, èrshǒude

used to (do sth.) (id.) 曾经做过 céngjīng zuò
  guo

used to (sth.) (adj.) 习惯于 xíguàn yú

useful (adj.) 有用的 yǒuyòngde

usually (adv.) 通常, 往往 tōngcháng,
  wǎngwǎng

V

vacant (adj.) 空的 kōngde

vacation (n.) 假期 jiàqī

valley (n.) 山谷 shāngǔ

valuable (adj., n.) 有价值的; 贵重物品
  yǒujiàzhíde; guìzhòng wùpǐn

van (n.) 面包车 miànbāochē

vase (n.) 花瓶 huāpíng

vegetable(s) (n.) 蔬菜 shūcài

velvet (adj.) 柔软的 róuruǎnde

very (adv.) 很 hěn

very much (exp.) 非常 fēicháng

vest (n.) 背心 bèixīn

view (n.) 风景, 观点 fēngjǐng, guāndiǎn

village (n.) 村子 cūnzi

visa (n.) 签证 qiānzhèng

visit (n., v.) 访问 fǎngwèn

visitor (n.) 访客 fǎngkè

vocabulary (n.) 词汇 cíhuì

volunteer (n.) 志愿者 zhìyuànzhě

vote (v.) 投票 tóupiào

W

waist (n.) 腰 yāo

wait (v.) 等 děng

waiter/waitress (n.) 服务员 fúwùyuán

wake up (v.) 醒来 xǐng lái

walk (go on foot) (v.) 步行 bùxíng

walk (take a walk) (id.) 散步 sànbù

wallet (n.) 钱包 qiánbāo

want (v.) 要 yào

war (n.) 战争 zhànzhēng

warm (adj.) 温暖的 wēnnuǎnde

wash (v.) 洗 xǐ

watch (n., v.) 手表; 观看 shǒubiǎo; guānkàn

water (n.) 水 shuǐ

water buffalo (n.) 水牛 shuǐniú

waterfall (n.) 瀑布 pùbù

way (n.) 方式, 办法 fāngshì, bànfǎ

way of life (n.) 生活方式 shēnghuó fāngshì

we (pron.) 我们 wǒmen

weak (adj.) 弱的 ruòde

wear (a cap or hat) (v.) 戴 dài

wear (clothes) (v.) 穿 chuān

198

weather (n.) 天气 tiānqì

wedding (n.) 婚礼 hūnlǐ

week (n.) 星期 xīngqī

weekend (n.) 周末 zhōumò

weigh (I weigh …) (v.) 重量为 zhòngliàng
 wéi

welcome (n., v.) 欢迎 huānyíng

well (adv.) 好地 hǎode

west (n.) 西方, 西部 xīfāng, xībù

Western (adj.) 西方的 Xīfāngde

Westerner (n.) 西方人 Xīfāngrén

wet (adj.) 潮湿的 cháoshīde

what (pron.) 什么 shénme

what about (id.) 又怎样 yòu zěnyàng

when (adv.) 什么时候 shénme shíhou

where (adv.) 在哪儿 zài nǎr

while (conj.) 当…时 dāng...shí

white (adj.) 白色的 báisède

who (pron.) 谁 shuí

wholesale (n.) 批发 pīfā

why (adv.) 为什么 wèishénme

wide (adj.) 宽的 kuānde

wide awake (adj.) 大醒 dà xǐng

widow (n.) 寡妇 guǎfu

widower (n.) 鳏夫 guānfu

wife (n.) 妻子 qīzi

win (v.) 赢, 胜 yíng, shèng

window (n.) 窗子 chuāngzi

windy (adj.) 有风的 yǒufēngde

winter (n.) 冬天 dōngtiān

wise (adj.) 明智的 míngzhìde

with (prep.) 和, 跟 hé, gēn

woman (n.) 女人 nǚrén

wonderful (adj.) 奇妙的 qímiàode

wood (firewood) (n.) 木柴 mùchái

woods (forest) (n.) 树林 shùlín

word (n.) 词 cí

work (n., v.) 工作 gōngzuò

work out (v.) 锻炼 duànliàn

world (n.) 世界 shìjiè

worse (adj.) 更坏的 gèng huài de

wrap (up) (v.) 包, 结束 bāo, jiéshù

write (v.) 写 xiě

wrong (adj.) 错误的 cuòwùde

Y

year (n.) 年 nián

yellow (adj.) 黄色的 huángsède

yes (adv.) 是, 对 shì, duì

yesterday (adv., n.) 昨天 zuótiān

yet (adv.) 仍, 还 réng, hái

you (pron.) 你 nǐ

your (adj.) 你的 nǐde

young (adj.) 年轻的 niánqīngde

younger than (adj.) 比…小 bǐ...xiǎo

your (pron.) 你的 nǐde

Z

zipper (n.) 拉链 lāliàn

zodiac (n.) 黄道 huángdào

zoo (n.) 动物园 dòngwùyuán

PHRASEBOOK

GREETINGS

Hi!
你 好 !
Nǐ hǎo!

你好 nǐ hǎo ! is the most common form of
greeting in Chinese. It can be used any time
during the day and on any occasion, formal or
informal. It does not require any specific
answer except 你好 nǐ hǎo in return.

Hello!
您 好 !
Nín hǎo!

您 nín is a polite form of 你 nǐ, similar to *vous*
in French and *usted* in Spanish. It is used
primarily in the northern part of China by a
younger person to an older person or between
strangers irrespective of age. If the use of 您
nín turns out to be too complicated resulting
from the consideration of age, rank and status
of the person spoken to, you may just stick to
你 nǐ on all the occasions. People won't get
offended being addressed 你 nǐ instead of 您
nín by foreigners.

A: How are you?
    你 好 吗 ?
    Nǐ hǎo ma?

B: <u>I am fine</u>. What about you?
<u>我 很 好</u>。你 呢？
<u>Wǒ hěn hǎo</u>. Nǐ ne?

A: I'm fine too.
我 也 很 好。
Wǒ yě hěn hǎo.

- Not bad   不错   bú cuò
- So-so   马马虎虎   mǎma hūhu

I haven't seen you for a long time. How are you?
好 久 不 见，你 好 吗？
Hǎo jiǔ bú jiàn, nǐ hǎo ma?

你好吗 nǐ hǎo ma is used to inquire about the well-being of the other person and it requires a specific answer.

A: How is your <u>father</u>?
你 <u>爸爸</u> 好 吗？
Nǐ <u>bàba</u> hǎo ma?

B: He is fine.
他 很 好。
Tā hěn hǎo.

B: How about your mother?
你 妈妈 呢？
Nǐ māma ne?

A: She is fine, too.
她 也 很 好。
Tā yě hěn hǎo.

206

- husband   先生   xiānsheng
- wife   太太   tàitai
- Miss   小姐   xiǎojiě

There is no distinction in pronunciation in Chinese between *he* and *she*. Both are pronounced tā, but they are represented by different characters in writing: 他 (he) and 她 (she).

How are you?
你 怎么样？
Nǐ zěnmeyàng?

怎么样 zěnmeyàng is a colloquial expression. It can be responded to by the same expressions in reply to 你好吗 nǐ hǎo ma.

How is your <u>business</u>?
你的 <u>生意</u> 怎么样？
Nǐde <u>shēngyì</u> zěnmeyàng?

- work   工作   gōngzuò
- study   学习   xuéxí
- health   身体   shēntǐ

Good morning!
你 早！
Nǐ zǎo!

Good morning!
早上　　好！
Zǎoshang hǎo!

Good afternoon!
下午　好！
Xiàwǔ hǎo!

Good evening!
晚上　　好！
Wǎnshang hǎo!

Good night!
晚　安！
Wǎn ān!

Welcome!
欢迎！
Huāngyíng!

ASKING NAMES

A: What is your last name?
　您　贵　姓？
　Nín guì xìng?

B: My last name is Li.
　我　姓　李。
　Wǒ xìng Lǐ.

In China, family names are considered more important than given names. For this reason, three things are to be noted. First, family names precede given names in Chinese, which is the exact reverse of the practice in Western languages. Second, when used with a title, the family name precedes the title, again the reverse of the practice in Western languages. Third, people almost always ask each other's family names when they meet for the first time and 您贵姓 nín guì xìng is the most frequently used question. In this polite and formal expression, 贵 guì is an honorific, meaning *honorable* or *respectable*. The whole question literally means *what is your respectable family name*?

A: What is your last name?
　你 姓　什么？
　Nǐ xìng shénme?

B: My last name is Huang.

209

我　姓　　黄。
Wǒ xìng Huáng.

您贵姓 nín guì xìng is usually used when the interlocutor is an adult or a superior. When an adult asks a youngster or when the speaker asks the family name of a third person who is not present, 你姓什么 nǐ xìng shénme is usually used.

A: What is your name?
　　你　叫　什么　名字?
　　Ni jiào shénme míngzi?
B: My name is Wang Zhong.
　　我　叫　王　　中。
　　Wǒ jiào Wáng Zhōng.

A: What is the name of your girlfriend?
　　你的　女朋友　　叫　什么　名字?
　　Nǐde　nǚpéngyou jiào shénme míngzi?
B: Her name is Li Hua.
　　她　叫　李华。
　　Tā jiào Lǐ Huá.

The exact meaning of 名字 míngzi depends on the context or listener's interpretation or preference. 名字 míngzi can be the full name or the given name alone, similar to *name* in *what's your name* in English. This question form is most useful because it can be used not only to ask people's names, but also to ask the names of places and things. It is advisable therefore for foreigners to stick to this expression whenever they want to ask people's names.

The most common surname in China, and in the entire world for the matter, is 李 Lǐ. There are approximately 100 million people in China and overseas with this surname. Other common surnames include 王 Wáng, 张 Zhāng, 赵 Zhào, 陈 Chén, 杨 Yáng, 吴 Wú, 刘 Liú, 黄 Huáng, 周 Zhōu. According to some statistics, the surname of the author of the book, 何 hé, ranks the eighteenth most common surname in China.

INTRODUCTIONS

This is my <u>mother</u>.
这 是 我 <u>妈妈</u>。
Zhè shì wǒ <u>māma</u>.

- father   爸爸   bàba
- older brother   哥哥   gēge
- younger brother   弟弟   dìdi
- older sister   姐姐   jiějie
- younger sister   妹妹   mèimei
- boyfriend   男朋友   nánpéngyou
- girlfriend   女朋友   nǚpéngyou

This is my colleague.
这 是 我的 同事。
Zhè shì wǒde tóngshì.

This is our teacher.
这 是 我们的 老师。
Zhè shì wǒmende lǎoshī.

The possessive marker 的 de is often omitted
after the personal pronouns 我 wǒ (I), 你 nǐ
(you), 他 tā (he) when what follows is a
person or place. This 的 de cannot be omitted
when what follows is a physical object. The
omission of 的 de usually takes place when
what follows is a person or place closely
related to the personal pronoun, particularly

family members and places the personal
pronoun is affiliated with.

A: This is <u>Miss</u> Zhang. This is Mr.
Wang.
这 是 张　<u>小姐</u>。 这 是
Zhè shì Zhāng <u>Xiǎojie</u>. Zhè shì
王　先生。
Wáng Xiānsheng.
B: It's a pleasure to know you.
认识 你, 我 很　高兴。
Rènshi nǐ, wǒ hěn gāoxìng.
C: It's also a pleasure to know
you.
认识 你, 我 也 很　高兴。
Rènshi nǐ, wǒ yě hěn gāoxìng.

- wife, Mrs.   太太   tàitai
- Ms., Madame   女士   nǚshì
- manager   经理   jīnglǐ
- director   主任   zhǔrèn

Both 先生 xiānsheng and 太太 tàitai have
double meanings. 先生 xiānsheng can mean
Mr. as well as *husband* and 太太 tàitai can
mean *Mrs.* as well as *wife*. When using these
address forms with the family name, the rule
is: the name precedes the title, instead of
following it as in English. Examples are 王先
生 Wáng Xiānsheng and 李小姐 Lǐ Xiǎojie.
太太 tàitai is not used very often to address

213

people because it is difficult to determine if the addressee is married or not and even if the addressee is married, she may still prefer to be addressed as 小姐 xiǎojie. Another reason that 太太 tàitai is not often used as an address form is that women in contemporary China do not take their husbands' family names after their marriage. To use 太太 tàitai after a woman's own name is therefore not appropriate. On formal occasions, the term 女士 nǚshì is often used to address a woman, married or unmarried. In addition, occupational names such as 经理 jīnglǐ (manager), 主任 zhǔrèn (director) and 校长 xiàozhǎng (principal) can be used as titles to address people.

Let me introduce myself.
我 来 介绍 一下 我 自己。
Wǒ lái jièshào yíxià wǒ zìjǐ.

This is my business card.
这 是 我的 名片。
Zhè shì wǒde míngpiàn.

A: Where do you work?
你 在 哪儿工作?
Nǐ zài nǎr gōngzuò?
B: I work for a <u>telephone company</u>.
我 在 <u>电话 公司</u> 工作。
Wǒ zài <u>diànhuà gōngsī</u> gōngzuò.

214

- bank   银行   yínháng
- barber's   理发店   lǐfàdiàn
- factory   工厂   gōngchǎng
- hospital   医院   yīyuàn
- lab   实验室   shíyànshì
- publisher   出版社   chūbǎnshè
- school   学校   xuéxiào
- store   商店   shāngdiàn
- trading company   贸易公司   màoyì gōngsī

A: What work do you do?
你 做 什么 工作？
Nǐ zuò shénme gōngzuò?

B: I am a teacher.
我 是 老师。
Wǒ shì lǎoshī.

- accountant   会计   kuàijì
- administrator   行政人员   xíngzhèng rényuán
- architect   建筑师   jiànzhùshī
- artist   艺术家   yìshùjiā
- attendant   服务员   fúwùyuán
- businessman   商人   shāngrén
- carpenter   木匠   mùjiang
- civil servant   公务员   gōngwùyuán
- clerk   职员   zhíyuán
- computer programmer   电脑程序师   diànnǎo chéngxùshī

215

INTRODUCTIONS

- designer 设计师 shèjìshī
- diplomat 外交官 wàijiāoguān
- doctor 医生 yīshēng
- driver 司机 sījī
- economist 经济学家 jīngjìxuéjiā
- engineer 工程师 gōngchéngshī
- farmer 农民 nóngmín
- lawyer 律师 lǜshī
- mechanic 修理工 xiūlǐgōng
- nurse 护士 hùshì
- pilot 飞行员 fēixíngyuán
- policeman 警察 jǐngchá
- professor 教授 jiàoshòu
- reporter 记者 jìzhě
- sales clerk 售货员 shòuhuòyuán
- secretary 秘书 mìshū
- scientist 科学家 kēxuéjiā
- worker 工人 gōngrén
- writer 作家 zuòjiā

THANK YOU

A: Thank you.
谢谢。
Xièxie
B: <u>You are welcome</u>.
<u>不谢</u>。
<u>Bùxiè</u>.

- Don't mention it   不用谢   Bú yòng xiè
- It's all right   不客气   Bú kèqi
- My pleasure   没事   Méishì

Many thanks.
多   谢。
Duō xiè

Thank you very much.
非常   感谢。
Fēicháng gǎnxiè.

Thank you for your <u>help</u>.
谢谢   你的 <u>帮助</u>。
Xièxie nǐde <u>bāngzhù</u>.

- coming   光临   guānglín
- concern   关心   guānxīn
- gift   礼物   lǐwù
- letter   来信   láixìn

217

LEAVE-TAKING

Good-bye!
再见！
Zàijiàn!

See you tomorrow!
明天　　见！
Míngtiān jiàn!

See you in school!
学校　　见！
Xuéxiào jiàn!

See you later.
回头　见。
Huítóu jiàn.

See you in a little while.
一会儿 见。
Yíhuìr　jiàn.

Welcome next time.
欢迎　　再 来。
Huānyíng zài lái.

Hope to see you soon.
希望　　我们　很 快　会 再
Xīwàng wǒmen hěn kuài huì zài
见面。
jiànmiàn.

218

It's getting late. I must be going.
时间　不早　了，我　该　走了。
Shíjiān bù zǎo le,　wǒ gāi zǒu le.

I must be going.
我　得　走　了。
Wǒ děi zǒu le.

I must be going.
我　必须　走　了。
Wǒ bìxū zǒu le.

Please stay a little longer.
请　再　坐　一会儿　吧。
Qǐng zài zuò yíhuìr　ba.

I really must say goodbye.
我　真的　　要　说　　再见　了。
Wǒ zhēnde yào shuō zàijiàn le.

When the guest indicates his or her intention
to leave, it is customary for the host to ask him
or her to stay a little longer. The particle 吧 ba
in the sentence indicates suggestion.

Please take care.
请　慢　走。
Qǐng màn zǒu.

Please take care.
请　多　保重。
Qǐng duō bǎozhòng.

LEAVE-TAKING

Bon voyage!
一 路 平安!
Yí lù píng'ān!

Have a nice journey!
一 路 顺风!
Yí lù shùnfēng!

The last two expressions are used to bid
farewell to a friend who is going on a long
journey.

NUMBERS & MEASURES

- one 一 yī
- two 二 èr
- three 三 sān
- four 四 sì
- five 五 wǔ
- six 六 liù
- seven 七 qī
- eight 八 bā
- nine 九 jiǔ
- ten 十 shí

- eleven 十一 shíyī
- twelve 十二 shí'èr
- thirteen 十三 shísān
- fourteen 十四 shísì
- fifteen 十五 shíwǔ
- sixteen 十六 shíliù
- seventeen 十七 shíqī
- eighteen 十八 shíbā
- nineteen 十九 shíjiǔ

- twenty 二十 èrshí
- thirty 三十 sānshí
- forty 四十 sìshí
- fifty 五十 wǔshí
- sixty 六十 liùshí
- seventy 七十 qīshí

- eighty   八十   bāshí
- ninety   九十   jiǔshí

- twenty-one   二十一   èrshíyī
- forty-three   四十三   sìshísān
- eighty-seven   八十七   bāshíqī

- hundred   百   bǎi
- thousand   千   qiān
- ten thousand   万   wàn
- hundred thousand   十万   shíwàn
- million   百万   bǎiwàn
- ten million   千万   qiānwàn
- hundred million   亿   yì

a hundred and fifty-four
一 百 五十 四
yì bǎi wǔshí sì

three thousand nine hundred and sixty-eight
三 千 九百 六十 八
sān qiān jiǔ bǎi liùshí bā

sixteen thousand three hundred seventy-six
一 万 六 千 三百 七十 六
yí wàn liù qiān sān bǎi qīshí liù

eight million
八 百万
bā bǎiwàn

222

twenty million

二 千万

èr qiānwàn

The number one is pronounced in the first tone (yī) when used as a pure number as in telephone numbers, ID numbers, zip codes, etc. When used in conjunction with a classifier and consequently a noun to indicate its quantity, it is pronounced in the second tone (yí) when followed by a fourth tone word, and in the fourth tone (yì) when followed by a first, second, third or neutral tone.

I have a Chinese book.

我 有 一 本 中文 书。

Wǒ yǒu yì běn Zhōngwén shū.

You have three Chinese friends.

你 有 三 个 中国 朋友。

Nǐ yǒu sān ge Zhōngguó péngyou.

She bought four movie tickets.

她 买 了 四 张 电影 票。

Tā mǎi le sì zhāng diànyǐng piào.

My mom gave me two sweaters.

我 妈妈 给 了 我 两 件 毛衣。

Wǒ māma gěi le wǒ liǎng jiàn máoyī.

Notice that whenever we use a number with a noun to indicate its quantity, we need to use a classifier, such as 本 běn, 个 ge，张 zhāng and

件 jiàn above. Refer to *A Brief Chinese Grammar* in the introductory section for more information.

• the first	第一	dìyī
• the second	第二	dì'èr
• the third	第三	dìsān
• the hundredth	第一百	dìyībǎi

It is quite easy to form ordinal numbers in Chinese. All you need to do is to prefix 第 dì to any cardinal number.

• half	半	bàn
• a quarter	四分之一	sì fēn zhī yī
• one-third	三分之一	sān fēn zhī yī
• two point five	两点五	liǎng diǎn wǔ
• one percent	百分之一	bǎi fēn zhī yī
• kilometer	公里	gōnglǐ
• meter	米	mǐ
• ten centimeters	分米	fēnmǐ
• centimeter	厘米	lǐmǐ
• millimeter	毫米	háomǐ
• mile	英里	yīnglǐ
• kilogram	公斤	gōngjīn
• gram	克	kè
• pound	英镑	yīngbàng
• ounce	盎司	àngsī
• gallon	加仑	jiālún
• liter	升	shēng

FAMILY

A: How many people are there in your
family?
你 家 有 几 口 人?
Nǐ jiā yǒu jǐ kǒu rén?

B: There are four people in my family.
我 家 有 四 口 人。
Wǒ jiā yǒu sì kǒu rén.

In most cases, the classifier 个 (ge) is used for
people (e.g. older brother, teacher, student,
doctor and lawyer) when they are preceded by
a number such as *three people*, *four teachers*,
or *two hundred students*. However, when we
talk about the number of people in a family,
we always use the classifier 口 (kǒu) instead.
For example: 我家有五 口人 (wǒ jiā yǒu wǔ
kǒu rén). The word 口 (kǒu) means *mouth* in
literary Chinese. When used for the number of
people in the family, it actually implies the
family has a certain number of mouths to feed.

A: Who are they?
他们 是 谁?
Tāmen shì shúi?

B: They are my wife, son, daughter and
myself.
他们 是 我 太太、 我 儿子、 我
Tāmen shì wǒ tàitai、 wǒ érzi、 wǒ
女儿 和 我。
nǚ'ér hé wǒ.

A: Does your wife work?

你太太 工作 吗？

Nǐ tàitai gōngzuò ma?

B: Yes, she does/No, she doesn't.

工作/ 不 工作。

Gōngzuò/Bù gōngzuò.

A: Do you have children?

你 有 孩子 吗？

Nǐ yǒu háizi ma?

B: Yes/No.

有/ 没 有。

Yǒu/Méi yǒu.

A: How many children do you have?

你们 有 几个 孩子？

Nǐmen yǒu jǐ ge háizi?

B: We have one daughter.

我们 有 一 个 女儿。

Wǒmen yǒu yí ge nǚér.

A: What school does your son attend?

你的 儿子 在 哪儿 读书？

Nǐde érzi zài nǎr dúshū?

B: My child is studying at <u>primary school</u>.

我的 儿子 在 <u>小学</u> 读书。

Wǒde érzi zài <u>xiǎoxué</u> dúshū.

- middle school   中学   zhōngxué
- university   大学   dàxué

A: Are you married?
    你 结婚 了 吗？
    Nǐ jiéhūn le ma?
B: Yes, I am/Not yet.
    结 了/还 没有。
    Jié le/Hái méiyou.

I am single.
我 是 单身。
Wǒ shì dānshēn.

I'm divorced.
我 离婚 了。
Wǒ líhūn le.

I'm separated from my wife.
我 和 我的 太太 分居 了。
Wǒ hé wǒde tàitai fēnjū le.

TIME

DIVISION OF THE DAY

• morning	早上	zǎoshang
• morning	上午	shàngwǔ
• noon	中午	zhōngwǔ
• afternoon	下午	xiàwǔ
• evening	晚上	wǎnshang
• night	夜里	yèlǐ
• daytime	白天	báitiān

DAYS

• day	天	tiān
• today	今天	jīntiān
• yesterday	昨天	zuótiān
• tomorrow	明天	míngtiān
• three days ago	三天前	sāntiān qián
• in four days	四天后	sìtiān hòu
• past	过去	guòqù
• now	现在	xiànzài
• future	将来	jiānglái
• time	时间	shíjiān
• hour	小时	xiǎoshí
• minute	分钟	fēnzhōng
• o'clock	点	diǎn
• watch	手表	shǒubiǎo
• clock	钟	zhōng

228

A: What's the time?
现在　是　几点/ 现在　是　什么
Xiànzài shì jǐ diǎn/xiànzài shì shénme
时间？
shíjiān?
B: It is nine o'clock.
现在　是　九　点。
Xiànzài shì jiǔ diǎn.

- 8 a.m.　　早上8点　　zǎoshang bā diǎn
- 8 p.m.　　晚上8点　　wǎnshàng bā diǎn
- 3 p.m.　　下午3点　　xiàwǔ sān diǎn
- 10 a.m.　 上午10点　 shàngwǔ shí diǎn

DAYS OF THE WEEK

- week　　　　星期　　　xīngqī
- Monday　　　星期一　　xīngqī yī
- Tuesday　　 星期二　　xīngqī èr
- Wednesday　 星期三　　xīngqī sān
- Thursday　　星期四　　xīngqī sì
- Friday　　　 星期五　　xīngqī wǔ
- Saturday　　 星期六　　xīngqī liù
- Sunday　　　星期天　　xīngqī tiān
- weekday　　 周日　　　zhōurì
- weekend　　 周末　　　zhōumò

A: What day is today?
今天　星期　几？
Jīntiān xīngqī jǐ?

B: Today is Monday/Tuesday/Wednesday/
Thursday/Friday/Saturday/Sunday.
今天　星期　一/二/三/四/五/　六/天。
Jīntiān xīngqi yī/ èr/sān/sì/ wǔ/liù/tiān.

MONTHS

- month   月   yuè
- January   一月   yí yuè
- February   二月   èr yuè
- March   三月   sān yuè
- April   四月   sì yuè
- May   五月   wǔ yuè
- June   六月   liù yuè
- July   七月   qī yuè
- August   八月   bā yuè
- September   九月   jiǔ yuè
- October   十月   shí yuè
- November   十一月   shíyī yuè
- December   十二月   shíèr yuè

A: What month is it?
现在　是 几月？
Xiànzài shì jǐ yuè?

B: It is May.
现在　是 五 月。
Xiànzài shì wǔ yuè.

A: What is the date today?
今天　是 几月 几号？
Jīntiān shì jǐ yuè jǐ hào?

B: Today is October 8.
今天 是 十 月 八 号。
Jīntiān shì shí yuè bā hào.

YEARS

- year　　　　　年　　　nián
- this year　　今年　　jīnnián
- last year　　去年　　qùnián
- next year　　明年　　míngnián

A: When were you born?
你 是 哪年 出生 　的?
Nǐ shì nǎ nián chūshēng de?
B: I was born on November 4, 1975.
我 是 1 9 7 5 年 11 月 4
Wǒ shì yī jiǔ qī wǔ nián shíyī yuè sì
号 出生 　的。
hào chūshēng de.

DIRECTIONS & POSITIONS

A: Excuse me, how do I go to the
downtown area?
请问， 我 怎么 去市 中心?
Qǐngwèn, wǒ zěnme qù shì zhōngxīn?

B: You can go by Subway #1 or Bus #4.
你可以坐 一 号 地铁， 也可以坐
Nǐ kěyǐ zuò yí hào dìtiě， yě kěyǐ zuò
四 路公共 汽车。
sì lù gōnggòng qìchē.

A: Excuse me, how do I go to the
Shanghai Museum?
请问， 去上海 博物馆
Qǐngwèn, qù Shànghǎi bówùguǎn
怎么 走?
zěnme zǒu?

B: Go straight along this street.
沿 着 这 条 街 一直 走。
Yán zhe zhè tiáo jiē yìzhí zǒu.

Go along this street and turn <u>left</u> at the second
intersection.
沿 着 这条 路向 前 走，在
Yán zhe zhè tiáo lù xiàng qián zǒu, zài
第二个 路口 向 <u>左</u> 转。
dì èr ge lùkǒu xiàng <u>zuǒ</u> zhuǎn.

- right 右 yòu
- east 东 dōng

232

- west   西   xī
- south   南   nán
- north   北   běi

A: Excuse me, where is the American Consulate?

请问， 美国 领事馆 在

Qǐngwèn, Měiguó Lǐngshìguǎn zài

哪儿？

nǎr?

B: Go across the street. Walk straight for 100 meters and you will be at the American Consulate.

过 了马路， 往 前 走 100 米

Guò le mǎlù, wǎng qián zǒu yìbǎi mǐ

就 是 美国 领事馆。

jiù shì Měiguó Lǐngshìguǎn.

A: Is there a police station nearby?

附近 有 警察局 吗？

Fùjìn yǒu jǐngchájú ma?

B: Yes. You don't have to walk far when you turn right before you can find the police station.

有， 往 右 走 不远 就是

Yǒu, wǎng yòu zǒu bù yuǎn jiù shì

警察局。

jǐngchájú.

A: Excuse me, where can I find a
   bathroom?
   请问，　哪儿有　厕所？
   Qǐngwèn, nǎr yǒu cèsuǒ?
B: There is a bathroom on the third floor.
   三　楼　有　厕所。
   Sān lóu yǒu cèsuǒ.

Can you tell me what the name of this street is?
你　能　告诉　我　这条　街　叫
Nǐ néng gàosù wǒ zhè tiáo jiē jiào
什么　名字　吗？
shénme míngzi ma?

A: Excuse me, is the <u>train station</u> far
   from here?
   请问，　<u>火车站</u>　离 这儿远
   Qǐngwèn, <u>huǒchēzhàn</u> lí zhèr yuán
   吗？
   ma?
B: 火车站/　离这儿很　近。
   huǒchēzhàn lí zhèr hěn jìn.

- airport　　　飞机场　　feijīchǎng
- bank　　　　银行　　　yínháng
- bus station　汽车站　　qìchēzhàn
- store　　　　商店　　　shāngdiàn

Excuse me, what (number) bus should I take to go to Beijing University?

请问，　去北京　大学　要　坐　几

Qǐngwèn, qù Běijīng Dàxué yào zuò jǐ

路汽车？

lù qìchē?

Can you tell where the stop for Bus #5 is?

你能　告诉我　五　路　汽车站　在

Nǐ néng gàosù wǒ wǔ lù qìchēzhàn zài

哪儿吗？

nǎr ma?

The movie theater is next to the post office.

电影院　　　在　邮局　的　旁边。

Diànyǐngyuàn zài yóujú de pángbiān.

The pharmacy is between the florist and the bakery.

药店　在　花店　和　面包店　　　的

Yàodiàn zài huādiàn hé miànbāodiàn de

中间。

zhōngjiān.

What's the address?

地址　是　什么？

Dìzhǐ shì shénme?

What's the building number?

门牌　　号码　是　多少？

Ménpái hàomǎ shì duōshao?

DIRECTIONS & POSITIONS

USEFUL WORDS & EXPRESSIONS

- alley   巷子   xiàngzi
- bridge   桥   qiáo
- church   教堂   jiàotáng
- hotel   旅馆   lǚguǎn
- information   问询处   wènxúnchù
- internet cafe   网吧   wǎngbā
- market   市场   shìchǎng
- mosque   清真寺   qīngzhēnsì
- one-way street   单行道   dānxíngdào
- street corner   街角   jiējiǎo
- square   广场   guǎngchǎng
- suburbs   郊区   jiāoqū
- university   大学   dàxué
- vegetable market 菜场   càichǎng
- village   村子   cūnzi

INVITATIONS

I'd like to invite you to <u>dinner</u>.
我 想 请 你 吃 <u>晚饭</u>。
Wǒ xiǎng qǐng nǐ chī <u>wǎnfàn</u>.

- drink coffee 喝咖啡 hē kāfēi
- go to an opera 看歌剧 kàn gējù
- see a movie 看电影 kàn diànyǐng

May I take you to lunch?
我 可以 请 你 吃 中饭 吗?
Wǒ kéyǐ qǐng nǐ chī zhōngfàn ma?

When someone uses 请 qǐng in inviting you, it
means that he or she will pay.

I'd like to invite you to attend our wedding.
我 想 邀请 你 参加 我们的
Wǒ xiǎng yāoqǐng nǐ cānjiā wǒmende
婚礼。
hūnlǐ.

My wife and I would like to invite you to visit
us this weekend.
我 和 我 太太 想 请 你 这 个
Wǒ hé wǒ tàitai xiǎng qǐng nǐ zhè ge
周末 来 作客。
zhōumò lái zuòkè.

237

Are you free tonight?

你 今天 晚上 　　有 空 　吗？

Nǐ jīntiān wǎnshang yǒu kòng ma?

Could you come to my house this Saturday evening?

你 星期六 晚上 　　能 不 能 　来

Nǐ xīngqīliù wǎnshang néng bu néng lái

我 家？

wǒ jiā?

Let's go and have a drink, shall we?

我们 　去 喝 一 杯， 好 不 好？

Wǒmen qù hē yì bēi, hǎo bu hǎo?

Let's go to dance tonight, shall we?

今天 　晚上 　　我们 　一起 去

Jīntiān wǎnshang wǒmen yìqǐ qù

跳舞， 好 吗？

tiàowǔ, hǎo ma?

Have dinner with us, would you?

跟 我们 　一起 吃饭， 好 　吗？

Gēn wǒmen yìqǐ chīfàn, hǎo ma?

We would love to come.

我们 　会 很 乐意 来 的。

Wǒmen huì hěn lèyì lái de.

I accept your invitation.

我 接受 你的 邀请。

Wǒ jiēshòu nǐde yāoqǐng.

238

I'd love to come, but I have another
appointment, so I can't make it.
我 很 想 来，但是 我 另
Wǒ hěn xiǎng lái, dànshì wǒ lìng
有 约，不 能 来。
yǒu yuē, bù néng lái.

Thank you for inviting me. I'll definitely come.
谢谢 你邀请 我，我 一定 来。
Xièxie nǐ yāoqǐng wǒ, wǒ yídìng lái.

HOSPITALITY

Come in, please.
请　进。
Qǐng jìn.

Sit down, please.
请　坐。
Qǐng zuò.

It's my treat today.
今天　我　请客。
Jīntiān wǒ qǐngkè.

You must let me pay this time.
这　次 你 一定　要　让　我
Zhè cì nǐ yídìng yào ràng wǒ
付 钱。
fù qián.

Please help yourself.
请　随便　用。
Qǐng suíbiàn yòng.

请　不要　客气。
Qǐng búyào kèqi.

Please eat a little more.
多　吃 一点儿。
Duō chī yìdiǎnr.

REQUESTS

Excuse me ...
请问，...
Qǐngwèn, ...

请问 qǐngwèn is a polite attention getter. It literally means *may I please ask*. However confusion may arise due to its frequent translation into *excuse me* in English. To translate the expression into *excuse me* is fine in this context, but to apply it to situations where you caused somebody inconvenience such as stepping on his toes is totally wrong. In other words, 请问 qǐngwèn is only equivalent to one of the meanings of *excuse me* in English. It is generally used when you would like to ask somebody a question.

A: May I come in?
    我 能 进来 吗?
    Wǒ néng jìn lái ma?
B: Sure.
    当然。
    Dāngrán.

Come in please.
请 进。
Qǐng jìn.

241

Please wait a second.
请　等　一下。
Qǐng děng yíxià.

Could you do me a favor?
你 能　帮　我 一 个 忙　吗？
Nǐ néng bāng wǒ yí ge máng ma?

I'd like to ask you for a favor.
我　想　请　你帮　个 忙。
Wǒ xiǎng qǐng nǐ bāng ge máng.

Could you point me the way?
你 能　给我 指 一下 路 吗？
Nǐ néng gěi wǒ zhǐ yíxià lù ma?

A: Could I ask you some questions?
　　我　可以　问　你 一些 问题
　　Wǒ kěyǐ　wèn nǐ yì xiē wèntí　　　吗？
　　ma?
B: Sure. Please feel free to ask.
　　当然，　　请　随便　问。
　　Dāngrán, qǐng suíbiàn wèn.

Could I bother you?
我　可以 打搅 你 一下 吗？
Wǒ kěyǐ dǎjiǎo nǐ yíxià ma?

Could you make way for me?
麻烦　你给我 让　个 路，行　吗？
Máfán nǐ gěi wǒ ràng ge lù,　xíng ma?

Can I smoke here?

我 可以 在 这儿 吸烟 吗？

Wǒ kěyǐ zài zhèr xīyān ma?

A: Are photos allowed here?

这儿允许 照相 吗？

Zhèr yǔnxǔ zhàoxiàng ma?

B: Yes. / No

可以. / 不 可 以/不 许/不 行。

Kěyǐ. / Bù kěyì/ Bù xǔ/ Bù xíng.

EMERGENCY

Help!
救命 啊！
Jiù mìng a!

Can you help me?
你 能 帮 我 吗？
Nǐ néng bāng wǒ ma?

Please summon the police for me.
请 帮 我 叫 警察。
Qǐng bāng wǒ jiào jǐngchá.

Please call the police.
请 帮 我 报警。
Qǐng bāng wǒ bàojǐng.

Is there a telephone nearby?
附近 有 电话 吗？
Fùjìn yǒu diànhuà ma?

What is the telephone number of the police department?
警察局 的 号码 是 多少？
Jǐngchájú de hàomǎ shì duōshao?

Please call the ambulance for me.
请 帮 我 叫 救护车。
Qǐng bāng wǒ jiào jiùhùchē.

It hurts here.
我 这儿 疼。
Wǒ zhèr téng.

Is there an international hospital here?
这儿 有 国际 医院 吗?
Zhèr yǒu guójì yīyuàn ma?

Is there any doctor here who can speak
English?
有 没 有 会 说 英语 的 医生?
Yǒu méi yǒu huì shuō Yīngyǔ de yīshēng?

Where is the pharmacy?
药房 在 哪儿?
Yàofáng zài nǎr?

Please take me to the hospital/ emergency
room.
请 送 我 去 医院/ 急诊室。
Qǐng sòng wǒ qù yīyuàn/jízhěnshì.

There is a car accident!
出 车祸 了!
Chū chēhuò le!

Someone got hurt.
有 人 受伤 了。
Yǒu rén shòushāng le.

Do not move!
不要 动!
Bùyào dòng!

245

Get away!
走 开!
Zǒu kāi!

I got lost.
我 迷 了 路。
Wǒ mí le lù.

I'm pregnant.
我 怀孕 了。
Wǒ huáiyùn le.

I am sick.
我 病 了。
Wǒ bìng le.

I was robbed.
我 被 抢 了。
Wǒ bèi qiǎng le.

There is a thief!
有 小偷!
Yǒu xiǎotōu!

Catch him!
抓 住 他!
Zhuā zhù tā!

My <u>car</u> was stolen.
我的 <u>车</u> 被 偷 了。
Wǒde <u>chē</u> bèi tōu le.

- camera 照相机 zhàoxiàngjī
- handbag 手提包 shǒutíbāo
- laptop 手提电脑 shǒutí diànnǎo
- money 钱 qián
- passport 护照 hùzhào
- travelers' 旅行支票 lǚxíng zhīpiào
  check
- wallet/purse 钱包 qiánbāo

They robbed my money.
他们 抢 了我的 钱。
Tāmen qiǎng le wǒde qián.

- leather bag 皮包 píbāo
- necklace 项链 xiàngliàn
- ring 戒指 jièzhi
- watch 手表 shǒubiǎo

I lost my passport.
我 丢 了护照。
Wǒ diū le hùzhào.

Danger!
危险！
Wēixiǎn!

Look out!
小心！
Xiǎoxīn!

EMERGENCY

Get out of the way!
让 开!
Ràng kāi!

I need to contact the embassy of my country.
我 要 跟 我 国 的 大使馆 联系。
Wǒ yào gēn wǒ guó de dàshǐguǎn liánxì.

I need an interpreter.
我 需要 翻译。
Wǒ xūyào fānyì.

USEFUL WORDS & EXPRESSIONS

• army	军队	jūnduì
• arson	纵火	zònghuǒ
• assassinate	暗杀	ànshā
• emergency	急救	jíjiù
• fire	火灾	huǒzāi
• get poisoned	中毒	zhòngdú
• hostages	人质	rénzhì
• military personnel	军人	jūnrén
• murder	谋杀	móushā
• pickpocket	扒手	páshǒu
• ransom	赎金	shújīn
• rape	强奸	qiángjiān
• robbery	抢劫	qiǎngjié
• theft	盗窃	dàoqiè
• war	战争	zhànzhēng

EMERGENCY

Frequently used telephone numbers in China:

114   telephone directory
119   fire
110   police

NATIONALITY

A: What is your nationality?
你 是 哪 国 人？
Nǐ shì nǎ guó rén?

B: I am <u>American</u>.
我 是 <u>美国人</u>。
Wǒ shì <u>Měiguórén</u>.

- Australian 澳大利亚人 Aòdàlìyàrén
- Austrian 奥地利人 Aòdìlìrén
- British 英国人 Yīnguórén
- Canadian 加拿大人 Jiā'nádàrén
- Chinese 中国人 Zhōngguórén
- Dutch 荷兰人 Hélánrén
- French 法国人 Fǎguórén
- German 德国人 Déguórén
- Indian 印度人 Yìndùrén
- Iranian 伊朗人 Yīlǎngrén
- Israeli 以色列人 Yǐsèlièrén
- Italian 意大利人 Yìdàlìrén
- Japanese 日本人 Rìběnrén
- Malaysian 马来西亚人 Mǎláixīyàrén
- Norwegian 挪威人 Nuówēirén
- Russian 俄国人 Éguórén
- Swiss 瑞典人 Ruìdiǎnrén

It is easy to form nationality terms in Chinese.
All you need to do is to add the word 人 (rén)
after the name of the country, such as the

above. To ask where someone is from, we use
你是哪国人 nǐ shì nǎ guó rén), which literally
means *which country person are you*.

A: Are you Chinese?
你 是 中国人 　　 吗?
Nǐ shì Zhōngguórén ma?
B: Yes/ No.
是 / 不 是。
Shì / Bú shì.

A: Where were you born?
你 是 在 什么 国家 出生 的?
Nǐ shì zài shénme guójiā chūshēng de?
B: I was born in <u>England</u>.
我 是 在 <u>英国</u> 出生 的。
Wǒ shì zài Yīngguó chūshēng de.

• Afghanistan	阿富汗	Āfùhàn
• Australia	澳大利亚	Àodàlìyà
• Austria	奥地利	Àodìlì
• Bangladesh	孟加拉	Mèngjiālā
• Bhutan	不丹	Bùdān
• Canada	加拿大	Jiā'nádà
• France	法国	Fǎguó
• Germany	德国	Déguó
• India	印度	Yìndù
• Sri Lanka	斯里兰卡	Sīlǐlánkǎ
• The Netherlands	荷兰	Hélán
• Iran	伊朗	Yīlǎng

- Ireland 爱尔兰 Aìrlán
- Israel 以色列 Yǐsèliè
- Italy 意大利 Yìdàlì
- Japan 日本 Rìběn
- Malaysia 马来西亚 Mǎláixīyà
- Myanmar 缅甸 Miǎndiàn
- Nepal 尼泊尔 Níbór
- New Zealand 新西兰 Xīnxīlán
- Norway 挪威 Nuówēi
- Russia 俄国 Éguó
- Spain 西班牙 Xībānyá
- Sweden 瑞典 Ruìdiǎn

I am an American citizen.
我 是 美国 公民。
Wǒ shì Měiguó gōngmín.

I am a foreigner.
我 是 外国人。
Wǒ shì wàiguórén.

LANGUAGE

A: Do you speak Chinese?
你 会 说　中文　　吗?
Nǐ huì shuō Zhōngwén ma?

B: Yes/ No/ A little bit.
会/ 不会/ 会 一点儿。
Huì/Bú huì/Huì yìdiǎnr.

A: What languages do you speak?
你 会 说　什么　语言?
Nǐ huì shuō shénme yǔyán?

B: I speak <u>Japanese</u>.
我 会 说　<u>日语</u>。
Wǒ huì shuō <u>Rìyǔ</u>.

- Arabic   阿拉伯语   Ālābóyǔ
- English   英语   Yīngyǔ
- French   法语   Fǎyǔ
- German   德语   Déyǔ
- Italian   意大利语   Yìdàlìyǔ
- Portuguese   葡萄牙语   Pútáoyáyǔ
- Russian   俄语   Éyǔ
- Spanish   西班牙语   Xībānyáyǔ

In all of these and other terms indicating
languages, 语 yǔ can be used interchangeably
with 文 wén. Both of them mean *language*.
An exception is with the Chinese language: 中

文 Zhōngwén, where 文 wén cannot be
substituted by 语 yǔ.

I only speak Chinese.
我　只　会　说　中文。
Wǒ zhǐ huì shuō Zhōngwén.

I only speak Mandarin. I don't speak
<u>Cantonese</u>.
我　只　会　说　普通话，　不　会　说
Wǒ zhǐ huì shuō Pǔtōnghuà, bú huì shuō
<u>广东话</u>。
<u>Guǎngdōnghuà</u>.

- Beijing dialect　　北京话　　Běijīnghuà
- Fujian dialect　　福建话　　Fújiànhuà
- Hakka dialect　　客家话　　Kèjiāhuà
- Shanghai dialect　上海话　　Shànghǎihuà

You speak very <u>good</u> Chinese.
你　中文　　说　得　很　<u>好</u>。
Nǐ Zhōngwén shuō de hěn <u>hǎo</u>.

- fluent　　　　　流利　　　liúlì
- idiomatic　　　　道地　　　dàodì

Excuse me, how to say "book" in Chinese?
请问，　　"book"用　中文　　怎么
Qǐngwèn, "book" yòng Zhōngwén zěnme
说？
shuō?

What does "diànnǎo" mean?
"电脑" 是 什么 意思?
"Diànnǎo" shì shénme yìsi?

Excuse me, how is this character pronounced?
请问, 这 个 字 怎么 发音?
Qǐngwèn, zhè ge zì zěnme fāyīn?

Excuse me, how to write this character?
请问, 这 个 字 怎么 写?
Qǐngwèn, zhè ge zì zěnme xiě?

Could you say it again?
你 能 再 说 一遍 吗?
Nǐ néng zài shuō yíbiàn ma?

Could you speak little slower?
您 能 慢 点儿 说 吗?
Nín néng màn diànr shuō ma?

Who can speak English?
谁 会 说 英语?
Shuí huì shuō Yīngyǔ?

I do not understand what you say.
我 不 懂 你的 话。
Wǒ bù dǒng nǐde huà.

Do you understand what I say?
你 听 得 懂 我的 话 吗?
Nǐ tīng de dǒng wǒde huà ma?

Let's talk in Chinese.
我们 用 中文 说 吧。
Wǒmen yòng Zhōngwén shuō ba.

Could you interpret for us?
你能 给我们 翻译 吗?
Nǐ néng gěi wǒmen fānyì ma?

I'd like to study Chinese.
我 想 学 中文。
Wǒ xiǎng xué Zhōngwén.

Could you teach me to speak Chinese?
你能 教 我 说 中文 吗?
Nǐ néng jiāo wǒ shuō Zhōngwén ma?

USEFUL WORDS & EXPRESSIONS

- conversation 会话 huìhuà
- grammar 语法 yúfǎ
- listen 听 tīng
- read 读 dú
- vocabulary 词汇 cíhuì

TELEPHONE

Hello!
喂！
Wéi!

Excuse me, who would you like to speak to?
请问，您找谁？
Qǐngwèn, nín zhǎo shúi?

Excuse me, who is it?
请问，您是谁？
Qǐngwèn, nín shì shúi?

I'd like to speak to Mr. Wang.
我找王先生。
Wǒ zhǎo Wáng Xiānsheng.

Is Mr. Wang in?
王先生在吗？
Wáng Xiānsheng zài ma?

Could I speak to your manager?
我能和你们的经理说话吗？
Wǒ néng hé nǐmende jīnglǐ shuōhuà ma?

Just a minute.
请等一下。
Qǐng děng yíxià.

257

He is not here right now.

他 现在　不 在。

Tā xiànzài bú zài.

Could I leave a message for him?

我 可以　给 他 留 话 吗?

Wǒ kěyǐ　gěi tā　liú huà ma?

Would you like to leave a message for him?

你 要　给 他 留 话　吗?

Nǐ yào gěi tā　liú huà ma?

Would you want me to ask him to call you back?

要　我　让　他 给 你 回 电话　吗?

Yào wǒ ràng tā gěi nǐ huí diànhuà ma?

Please ask him to call me back when he returns.

请　他 回来　后　给 我　打 电话。

Qǐng tā huí lái hòu gěi wǒ dǎ diànhuà.

What is your telephone number?

您的　电话　　号码　是 多少?

Nínde diànhuà hàomǎ shì duōshao?

My telephone number is 8335-9451.

我的　电话　　号码　是 8 3 3 5-

Wǒde diànhuà hàomǎ shì bā sān sān wǔ

9 4 5 1。

jiǔ sì wǔ yī.

258

Can I use this phone?
我 可以 用 一下 这 个 电话 吗?
Wǒ kéyǐ yòng yíxià zhè ge diànhuà ma?

Could you tell me how to use this phone card?
你 能 告诉 我 怎么 用 这 个
Nǐ néng gàosù wǒ zěnme yòng zhè ge
电话卡 吗?
diànhuàkǎ ma?

Could you tell me how to use <u>the pay phone</u>?
你 能 告诉 我 怎么 用 <u>公用</u>
Nǐ néng gàosù wǒ zěnme yòng <u>gōngyòng</u>
<u>电话</u> 吗?
<u>diànhuà</u> ma?

- coin-operated   投币电话   tóubì diànhuà
  telephone
- magnetic card   磁卡电话   cíkǎ diànhuà
  telephone

Do you have a telephone book?
你们 有 没 有 电话 号码 簿?
Nǐmen yǒu méi yǒu diànhuà hàomǎ bù?

The line is busy now.
现在 电话 占 线。
Xiànzài diànhuà zhàn xiàn.

The phone call got disconnected.
电话 断 了。
Diànhuà duàn le.

259

The phone is broken.
电话　坏 了。
Diànhuà huài le.

Please connect me to the translator.
请　给我　接 翻译。
Qǐng géi wǒ jiē fānyì.

Please hold on.
请　不 要　挂。
Qǐng bú yào guà.

APPOINTMENT

A: When can I come to see you?
我 什么 时候 可以来 见 你？
Wǒ shénme shíhou kěyǐ lái jiàn nǐ?

B: <u>You can come anytime.</u>
你 什么 时间 来 都 可以。
Nǐ shénme shíjiān lái dōu kěyǐ.

• You can come anytime.
你 随时 都 可以 来。
Nǐ suíshí dōu kěyǐ lái.

• Anytime between 7 and 9.
7 点 到 9 点 之间 的任何
Qī diǎn dào jiǔ diǎn zhījiān de rènhé
时间 都 可以。
shíjiān dōu kěyǐ.

什么时间 shénme shíjiān is similar to *what time* in English. It is used to ask a specific time. The answer must be a clock time, such as 7 o'clock or 8:30. 什么时候 shénme shíhou is similar to *when* in English in that the answer can be a clock time, or a general time such as *tomorrow*, *next week*, or even *next year*. Thus 什么时候 shénme shíhou can often be used in place of 什么时间 shénme shíjiān, but the reverse is not true when the expected answer is a general time.

261

A: I would like to come to see you. Do you have time this afternoon?
我 想　来 见 你，你今天
Wǒ xiǎng lái jiàn nǐ,　nǐ jīntiān
下午 有　时间　吗?
xiàwǔ yǒu shíjiān ma?

B: It's not good this afternoon. Can you come tomorrow morning?
今天　下午　不 行，你 明天
Jīntiān xiàwǔ bù xíng, nǐ míngtiān
上午　　能　来 吗?
shàngwǔ néng lái ma?

Are you free tonight?
你 今天　晚上　　有 空　吗?
Nǐ jīntiān wǎnshang yǒu kòng ma?

Are you busy tomorrow evening?
你明天　　晚上　　有 事 吗?
Nǐ míngtiān wǎnshang yǒu shì ma?

What time is good for you?
什么　　时间　对 你比较　方便?
Shénme shíjiān duì nǐ bǐjiào fāngbiàn?

FOOD & DRINK

I'm hungry
我 饿 了。
Wǒ è le.

I am thirsty.
我 渴 了。
Wǒ kě le.

Is there a Western/Chinese breakfast here?
这儿 有 西式/中式 早餐 吗?
Zhèr yǒu xīshì/zhōngshì zǎocān ma?

What do you want to eat?
你们 想 吃 什么?
Nǐmen xiǎng chī shénme?

Do you like to eat <u>Chinese food</u>?
你 喜欢 吃 <u>中国 菜</u> 吗?
Nǐ xǐhuan chī <u>Zhōngguó cài</u> ma?

- Cantonese cuisine   广东菜   Guǎngdōng cài
- Hunan cuisine   湖南菜   Húnán cài
- local flavor   地方菜   dìfang cài
- Sichuan cuisine   四川菜   Sìchuān cài
- Shanghai cuisine   上海菜   Shànghǎi cài

I am vegetarian.
我 只 吃 素。
Wǒ zhǐ chī sù.

I'm sorry. I don't eat meat.
对不起，我 不 吃 肉。
Duìbuqǐ, wǒ bù chī ròu.

I do not eat fish and seafood.
我 不吃 鱼 和 海鲜。
Wǒ bù chī yú hé hǎixiān.

Is this dish spicy?
这 个 菜 辣 吗?
Zhè ge cài là ma?

Please do not put MSG in the dish.
菜 里请 不要 放 味精。
Cài lǐ qǐng búyào fàng wèijīng.

What is this dish?
这 是 什么 菜?
Zhè shì shénme cài?

What would you like to drink?
你们 要 喝 点 什么?
Nǐmen yào hē diǎn shénme?

Please give me a glass of <u>ice water.</u>
请 给我 一杯 <u>冰 水</u>。
Qǐng gěi wǒ yì bēi <u>bīng shuǐ</u>.

- coffee   咖啡   kāfēi
- orange juice   橙汁   chéngzhī
- tea   茶   chá

Very delicious.
非常　好吃。
Fēicháng hǎochī.

Yummy indeed.
好吃　极了。
Hǎochī jíle.

It tastes very good.
味道　很　好。
Wèidào hěn hǎo.

The dish is too <u>salty</u>.
菜 太 <u>咸</u> 了。
Cài tài <u>xián</u> le.

- bland   淡   dàn
- sour   酸   suān
- spicy   辣   là
- sweet   甜   tián

Cheers!
干杯！
Gānbēi!

Please bring me some fruit.
请　给我 来　一点儿 水果。
Qǐng gěi wǒ lái yìdiǎnr shuǐguǒ

FOOD & DRINK

We've finished. Please give us the bill.
我们 吃 完 了，请 给 我们
Wǒmen chī wán le, qǐng gěi wǒmen
账单。
zhàngdān.

TYPES OF EATERIES

• cafeteria	餐厅	cāntīng
• coffee shop	咖啡馆	kāfēiguǎn
• fast-food restaurant	快餐店	kuàicāndiàn
• KFC	肯得基	Kěndéjī
• McDonald's	麦当劳	Màidāngláo
• mess hall	食堂	shítáng
• Pizza Hut	必胜客	Bìshèngkè
• restaurant	餐馆/饭馆	cānguǎn/ fànguǎn
• snack shop	小吃店	xiǎochīdiàn

TYPES OF MEALS

• boxed meal	盒饭	héfàn
• breakfast	早餐	zǎocān
	早饭	zǎofàn
• Chinese food	中餐	zhōngcān
• dinner	晚餐	wǎncān
	晚饭	wǎnfàn
• lunch	中餐	zhōngcān
	中饭	zhōngfàn
	午餐	wǔcān
	午饭	wǔfàn

FOOD & DRINK

- set meal   套餐   tàocān
- snack   小吃   xiǎochī
- Western food   西餐   xīcān

TYPICAL CHINESE FOOD

- diced chicken   宫爆鸡丁   gōngbào jīdīng
  with peppers
  and peanuts
- dumpling   饺子   jiǎozi
- fried pancake   油饼   yóubǐng
- Peking duck   北京烤鸭   Běijīng kǎoyā
- spicy tofu   麻婆豆腐   mápó dòufu
- spring roll   春卷   chūnjuǎn
- steamed bun   包子   bāozi
- steamed fish   清蒸鱼   qīngzhēngyú
- sweet and   咕老肉   gǔlǎo ròu
  sour pork
- sweet and   酸辣汤   suān là tāng
  sour soup
- wonton   馄饨   húntun

TYPICAL WESTERN FOOD

- bread   面包   miànbāo
- butter   牛油   niúyóu
- cereal   麦片   màipiàn
- cheese   奶酪   nǎilào
- hamburger   汉堡   hànbǎo
- hot dog   热狗   règǒu
- salad   沙拉   shālā
- sandwich   三明治   sānmíngzhì

FOOD & DRINK

- sausage · 香肠 · xiāngcháng
- spaghetti · 空心面 · kōngxīnmiàn
- steak · 牛排 · niúpái

NOODLES & RICE

- chow mein · 炒面 · chǎomiàn
- cooked rice · 米饭 · mǐfàn
- fried rice · 炒饭 · chǎofàn
- noodles · 面条 · miàntiáo
- porridge · 稀饭 · xīfàn

DRINKS & BEVERAGES

- apple juice · 苹果汁 · píngguǒzhī
- juice · 果汁 · guǒzhī
- lemon juice · 柠檬汁 · níngméngzhī
- milk · 牛奶 · niúnǎi
- orange juice · 橙汁 · chénzhī
- pineapple juice · 菠萝汁 · bōluózhī
- soy milk · 豆浆 · dòujiāng
- spring water · 矿泉水 · kuàngquánshuǐ
- yogurt · 酸奶 · suānnǎi

- beer · 啤酒 · píjiǔ
- champagne · 香槟酒 · xiāngbīnjiǔ
- red wine · 红酒 · hóngjiǔ
- saki · 米酒 · mǐjiǔ
- vodka · 伏特加 · fútèjiā
- white wine · 白酒 · báijiǔ
- whiskey · 威士忌 · wēishìjì

FOOD & DRINK

- wine 葡萄酒 pútáojiǔ

- black tea 红茶 hóngchá
- Coca Cola 可口可乐 kěkǒukělè
- green tea 绿茶 lǜchá
- ice tea 冰茶 bīngchá
- jasmine tea 花茶 huáchá
- Pepsi 百事可乐 bǎishìkělè
- soda 汽水 qìshuǐ
- Sprite 雪碧 xuěbì
- tea 茶 chá

HEALTHCARE

I am sick.
我 病 了。
Wǒ bìng le.

I'm not feeling well. I want to see the doctor.
我 不 舒服，我 要 看 医生。
Wǒ bù shūfu, wǒ yào kàn yīshēng.

Is there a hospital nearby?
附近 有 医院 吗?
Fùjìn yǒu yīyuàn ma?

Where is the nearest hospital?
离 这儿 最 近 的 医院 在 哪儿?
Lí zhèr zuì jìn de yīyuàn zài nǎr?

I think we'd better send him to hospital.
我 想 我们 应该 送 他去
Wǒ xiǎng wǒmen yīnggāi sòng tā qù
医院。
yīyuàn.

Please call the ambulance!
请 叫 救护车!
Qǐng jiào jiùhùchē!

I want to see a <u>doctor of internal medicine</u>.
我 要 看 内科 医生。
Wǒ yào kàn nèikē yīshēng.

270

- dentist   牙科医生   yákē yīshēng
- dermatologist   皮肤科医生   pífūkē yīshēng
- gynecologist   妇科医生   fùkē yīshēng
- oncologist   肿瘤医生   zhǒngliú yīshēng
- ophthalmo-logist   眼科医生   yǎnkē yīshēng
- orthopaedic surgery   骨科医生   gǔkē yīshēng
- pediatrician   小儿科医生   xiǎorkē yīshēng
- surgeon   外科医生   wàikē yīshēng
- urologist   泌尿科医生   mìniàokē yīshēng

Terms for doctors of various specialties are formed by adding 医生 to the name of the specialty such as 外科医生 wàikē yīshēng (surgeon), 内科医生 nèikē yīshēng (doctor of internal medicine).

What's wrong?
你 怎么 了？
Nǐ zěnme le?

A: What troubles you?
你 哪儿 不 舒服？
Nǐ nǎr　 bù shūfu?

B: I have a <u>headache</u>.
我 头 疼。
Wǒ <u>tóu téng</u>.

- allergy   过敏   guòmǐn
- diarrhea   拉肚子   lādùzi
- dizziness   头晕   tóuyūn
- fever   发烧   fāshāo
- sore throat   嗓子疼   sǎngzi téng
- spasm   痉挛   jìngluán
- stomachache   肚子疼   dùzi téng
- vomiting   呕吐   ǒutù
- pneumonia   肺炎   fèiyán

I want to vomit.
我 想 吐。
Wǒ xiǎng tù.

I cannot fall asleep.
我 睡 不 着 觉。
Wǒ shuì bù zháo jiào.

I'm pregnant.
我 怀孕 了。
Wǒ huáiyùn le.

Could you please dress this wound for me?
你 能 给 我 包扎 这 个 伤口 吗？
Nǐ néng gěi wǒ bāozā zhè ge shāngkǒu ma?

Please measure my blood pressure.
请　量　一下　我的　血压。
Qǐng liáng yíxià wǒde xuèyā.

I need to give you a <u>blood</u> test.
我　要　验　一下　你的　<u>血</u>。
Wǒ yào yàn yíxià nǐde <u>xuè</u>.

- stool　　大便　　dàbiàn
- urine　　小便　　xiǎobiàn

Do I need to be hospitalized?
我　要　住院　　吗？
Wǒ yào zhùyuàn ma?

When can I be discharged from hospital?
我　什么　　时候　能　　出院？
Wǒ shénme shíhou néng chūyuan?

Excuse me, is there a pharmacy nearby?
请问，　　附近　有　药房　　吗？
Qǐngwèn, fùjìn yǒu yàofáng ma?

Could you fill this prescription?
你　能　按　这　个　处方　　给　我
Nǐ néng àn zhè ge chǔfāng gěi wǒ
配　药　吗？
pèi yào ma?

I want medicine for a <u>cold</u>.
我　要　治　感冒　的　药。
Wǒ yào zhì <u>gǎnmào</u> de yào.

273

- constipation 便秘 biànmì
- diabetes 糖尿病 tángniàobìng
- headache 头疼 tóu téng
- stomachache 肚子疼 dùzi téng
- toothache 牙疼 yá téng

I want <u>painkillers</u>.
我 要 <u>止疼药</u>。
Wǒ yào <u>zhǐténgyào</u>.

- antibiotics 抗生素 kàngshēngsù
- aspirin 阿斯匹林 āsīpǐlín
- sleeping pills 安眠药 ānmiányào

What medicine is this?
这 是 什么 药?
Zhè shì shénme yào?

I am allergic to <u>dust</u>.
我 对 <u>灰尘</u> 过敏。
Wǒ duì <u>huīchén</u> guòmǐn.

- peanuts 花生 huāshēng
- penicillin 青霉素 qīngméisù
- perfume 香水 xiāngshuǐ
- pollen 花粉 huāfěn
- wheat 麦子 màizi

ADDITIONAL SYMPTOMS & DISEASES

• AIDS	爱滋病	àizībìng
• anemia	贫血	pínxuě
• appendicitis	盲肠炎	máng chángyán
• arthritis	关节炎	guānjiéyán
• asthma	哮喘	xiàochuǎn
• bacteria	细菌	xìjūn
• cancer	癌症	áizhèng
• cholera	霍乱	huòluàn
• cold	伤风	shāngfēng
• cough	咳嗽	késòu
• fatigue	疲倦	píjuàn
• food poisoning	食物中毒	shíwù zhòngdú
• fracture	骨折	gǔzhé
• gastritis	肠胃炎	chángwèiyán
• heart disease	心脏病	xīnzàngbìng
• indigestion	消化不良	xiāohuà bùliáng
• infection	发炎	fāyán
• infectious disease	传染病	chuánrǎnbìng
• heart failure	心脏衰竭	xīnzàng shuāijié
• high blood pressure	高血压	gāoxuěyā
• influenza	流行性感冒	liúxíngxìng gǎnmào

- insomnia 失眠 shīmián
- leprosy 麻风病 máfēngbìng
- malaria 疟疾 nüèji
- measles 麻疹 mázhěn
- polio 小儿 xiǎor
  麻痹症 mábìzhèng
- rheumatism 风湿症 fēngshīzhèng
- ringing in 耳鸣 ěrmíng
  the ear
- scarlet fever 腥红热 xīnghóngrè
- sexually 性病 xìngbìng
  transmitted
  disease
- smallpox 天花 tiānhuā
- tuberculosis 肺结核 fèijiéhé
- virus 病毒 bìngdú

- Chinese 中医 zhōngyī
  medicine
- acupuncture 针灸 zhēnjiǔ
- massage 推拿 tuī'ná
- herb medicine 中草药 zhōngcǎoyào

HOTEL & ACCOMMODATIONS

Can you recommend me a hotel?
你能　给我们　推荐　一家旅馆　吗？
Nǐ néng gěi wǒmen tuījiàn yì jiā lǚguǎn ma?

We'd like to stay in the downtown area.
我们　想　住　在　市中心。
Wǒmen xiǎng zhù zài shì zhōngxīn.

I want to stay in an inexpensive hotel.
我想　住一家不太贵的饭店。
Wǒ xiǎng zhù yì jiā bú tài guì de fàndiàn.

I'd like to book a room
我　想　订　一个房间。
Wǒ xiǎng dìng yí ge fángjiān.

I want a single room.
我　想　要　一个 <u>单人</u>　房间。
Wǒ xiǎng yào yí ge <u>dānrén</u> fángjiān.

- double room　双人房间　shuāngrén fángjiān
- standard room　标准间　biānzhǔnjiān
- suite　套间　tàojiān

I want a room with <u>two beds</u>.
我　想　要　一个有　<u>两　张　床</u>
Wǒ xiǎng yào yí ge yǒu <u>liǎng zhāng chuáng</u>的
房间。
de fángjiān.

277

- balcony   阳台   yángtái
- living room   客厅   kètīng
- single bed   单人床   dānrénchuáng
- telephone   电话   diànhuà
- TV   电视   diànshì

Is breakfast included?
包 不 包 早餐？
Bāo bu bāo zǎocān?

Does your hotel have a <u>restaurant</u>?
你们的 饭店 有 餐馆 吗？
Nǐmende fàndiàn yǒu <u>cānguǎn</u> ma?

- business center   商务中心   shāngwù zhōngxīn
- elevator   电梯   diàntī
- gym   健身房   jiànshēnfáng
- swimming pool   游泳池   yóuyǒngchí
- the barber's   理发室   lǐfàshì

Is there <u>air conditioning</u> in the room?
房间 里有 没 有 空调？
Fángjiān lǐ yǒu méi yǒu <u>kōngtiáo</u>?

- bar   酒吧   jiǔbā
- hot water   热水   rèshuǐ
- safe   保险箱   bǎoxiǎnxiāng

Please take my luggage to my room.
请 把 我的 行李 送 到 我的
Qǐng bǎ wǒde xíngli sòng dào wǒde
房间。
fángjiān.

This room is too cold.
这 个 房间 太 冷。
Zhè ge fángjiān tài lěng.

- dark   暗   àn
- dirty   脏   zāng
- hot   热   rè
- noisy   吵   chǎo
- small   小   xiǎo

Could you please give me a towel?
你 能 给我 一个 毛巾 吗?
Nǐ néng gěi wǒ yí ge máojīn ma?

- bath towel   浴巾   yùjīn
- blanket   毯子   tǎnzi
- coffee pot   咖啡壶   kāfēihú
- pillow   枕头   zhěntou

I need toilet paper.
我 需要 卫生纸。
Wǒ xūyào wèishēngzhǐ.

- clean bed sheet 干净的   gānjìngde
                   床单   chuángdān

- hanger   衣服架   yīfujià
- iron   熨斗   yùndǒu
- plug   插头   chātóu
- soup   肥皂   féizào
- toothpaste   牙膏   yágāo

Please take these clothes to the laundry room.
请 把 这 些 衣服 送 到 洗衣房。
Qǐng bǎ zhè xiē yīfu sòng dào xǐyīfáng.

Please take these clothes to iron.
请 把 这 些 衣服 拿去 熨 一下。
Qǐng bǎ zhè xiē yīfu ná qù yùn yíxià.

Please change my bed sheet.
请 更换 我的 床单。
Qǐng gēnghuàn wǒde chuángdān.

Please clean my room.
请 打扫 我的 房间。
Qǐng dǎsǎo wǒde fángjiān.

I'd like to check out.
我 要 退房。
Wǒ yào tuìfáng.

Can I pay with a credit card?
我 可以 用 信用卡 付款 吗?
Wǒ kěyǐ yòng xìnyòngkǎ fùkuǎn ma?

Several terms are used in China to refer to hotels and accommodations. The generic one is 旅馆 lǚguǎn (hotel), but actual hotels are usually called 饭店 fàndiàn, 酒店 jiǔdiàn or 宾馆 bīn'guǎn.

MONEY & BANKING

Where is the <u>Bank of China</u>?
<u>中国　　　银行</u>　在 哪儿?
<u>Zhōngguó Yínháng</u> zài nǎr?

• American Bank	美洲银行	Měizhōu Yínháng
• American Express Bank	美国运通银行	Měiguó Yùntōng Yínháng
• Chase Bank	大通银行	Dàtōng Yínháng
• CitiBank	花旗银行	Huāqí Yínháng
• Construction Bank	建设银行	Jiànshè Yínháng
• People's Bank of China	中国人民银行	Zhōngguó Rénmín Yínháng

Where is the nearest bank?
最　近 的 银行　在 哪儿?
Zuì jìn de yínháng zài nǎr?

A: Can you tell me where I can exchange U.S. dollars?
你 能　告诉 我 在 哪儿 能　换
Nǐ néng gàosù wǒ zài nǎr néng huàn
美元　　吗?
Měiyuán ma?

282

B: You can exchange at a bank or at a hotel.
你 可以在 银行　换，也 可以 在
Nǐ kěyǐ zài　yínháng huàn, yě kěyǐ　zài
饭店　换。
fàndiàn huàn.

I'd like to open an account.
我 想　开 一个 账户。
Wǒ xiǎng kāi yí ge zhànghù.

I'd like to make a deposit.
我 要 存 款。
Wǒ yào cún kuǎn.

I'd like to make a withdrawal.
我 要 取 款。
Wǒ yào qǔ kuǎn.

I'd like to cash this traveler's check.
我 想　兑换　这 张　旅行
Wǒ xiǎng duìhuàn zhè zhāng lǚxíng
支票。
zhīpiào.

Can you tell me how to use the ATM?
你 能　告诉 我 怎么　用　取款
Nǐ néng gàosù wǒ zěnme yòng qǔkuǎn
机 吗?
jī ma?

There are three monetary units in the Chinese currency 人民币 rénmínbì: 元 yuán/块 kuài, 角 jiǎo/毛 máo and 分 fēn. The difference between 元 yuán and 块 kuài, and between 角 jiǎo and 毛 máo is that 元 yuán and 角 jiǎo are formal and written expressions, whereas 块 kuài and 毛 máo are spoken and everyday forms. One 元 yuán/块 kuài consists of ten 角 jiǎo/毛 máo and one 角 jiǎo/ 毛 máo consists of ten 分 fēn in turn. Comparison should be made with the American monetary system where there are only two formal units: dollar and cent. We may say 99 cents in English, but we can never say 99 分 fēn in Chinese simply because there is an additional unit for ten cents in Chinese. The correct form of 99 cents in Chinese is 9 毛 máo 9 分 fēn.

USEFUL WORDS & EXPRESSIONS

• British pound	英镑	Yīngbàng
• Canadian dollar	加元	Jiāyuán
• Euro	欧元	Ōuyuán
• Hong Kong dollars	港币	Gǎngbì
• Japanese yen	日元	Rìyuán
• Ruble	卢布	Lúbù
• certificate of deposit	定期存款	dìngqí cúnkuǎn
• checking account	支票账户	zhīpiào zhànghù

- savings account   储蓄帐户   chúxù
  zhànghù

- banknotes   钞票   chāopiào
- cash   现款   xiànkuǎn
- change   零钱   língqián
- coin   硬币   yìngbì
- foreign currency   外币   wàibì

SHOPPING

Is there an antique store nearby?
附近 有 <u>古董 店</u> 吗？
Fùjìn yǒu gǔdǒng diàn ma?

- bakery 面包店 miànbāodiàn
- barber's 理发店 lǐfàdiàn
- beauty parlor 美容店 měiróngdiàn
- bookstore 书店 shūdiàn
- calligraphy and 字画店 zìhuàdiàn
  painting store
- candy store 糖果店 tángguǒdiàn
- clothing store 服装店 fúzhuāngdiàn
- department store 百货公司 bǎihuògōngsī
- drug store 药店 yàodiàn
- electronics store 电器店 diànqìdiàn
- florist's 花店 huādiàn
- fruit store 水果店 shuǐguǒdiàn
- grocery store 杂货店 záhuòdiàn
- hardware store 五金店 wǔjīndiàn
- jewelry store 珠宝店 zhūbǎodiàn
- optical store 眼镜店 yǎnjìngdiàn
- shoe store 鞋店 xiédiàn
- shopping center 购物中心 gòuwù
  zhōngxīn
- stationery store 文具店 wénjùdiàn
- supermarket 超级市 chāojí
  场 shìchǎng

286

- tailor's 裁缝店 cáiféngdiàn
- toy store 玩具店 wánjùdiàn
- watch store 钟表店 zhōngbiǎo diàn

Where can I find a gift store?
哪儿 有 礼品 店?
Nǎr yǒu lǐpǐn diàn?

Is it far from here?
离 这儿 远 吗?
Lí zhèr yuǎn ma?

What time do you open/close?
你们 几点 开门/ 关门?
Nǐmén jǐ diǎn kāimén/guānmén?

What would you like to buy?
你 要 买 什么?
Nǐ yào mǎi shénme?

I'm just looking.
我 只是 看看。
Wǒ zhǐshì kànkàn.

Please show me this.
请 把 这 个 拿给 我 看看。
Qǐng bǎ zhè ge ná gěi wǒ kànkan.

Do you ship?
你们 托运 吗?
Nǐmén tuōyùn ma?

Can you ship this to America?
你能 把这个 东西 运 到
Nǐ néng bǎ zhè ge dōngxi yùn dào
美国 吗?
Měiguó ma?

What's the brand of this camera?
这 个 照相机 是 什么 牌子 的?
Zhè ge zhàoxiàngjī shì shénme páizi de?

What country is this product made in?
这 个 产品 是 哪 国 货?
Zhè ge chǎnpǐn shì nǎ guó huò?

A: What material is this?
这 是 什么 料子 的?
Zhè shì shénme liàozi de?
B: This is <u>wool</u>.
这 是 <u>羊毛</u> 的。
Zhè shì <u>yángmáo</u> de.

- cloth   布   bù
- cotton   全棉   quánmián
- linen   麻   má
- polyester   化纤   huàqiān
- silk   丝   sī

Can you give me a discount?
你能 给我 打折 吗?
Nǐ néng gěi wǒ dǎzhé ma?

I can give you 10% off.
我 可以 给 你 打 九折。
Wǒ kěyǐ gěi nǐ dǎ jiǔzhé.

50% off	五折	wǔzhé
40% off	六折	liùzhé
30% off	七折	qīzhé
20% off	八折	bāzhé
10% off	九折	jiǔzhé

Would you make it a little even cheaper?
能 不能 再 便宜 一点儿?
Néng bu néng zài piányi yìdiǎnr?

I'll buy two. How much discount can you give me?
我 买 两 个, 你 能 便宜 多少?
Wǒ mǎi liǎng ge, nǐ néng piányi duōshao?

I don't want it.
我 不要。
Wǒ bú yào.

I want something cheaper.
我 要 便宜 一点 的。
Wǒ yào piányi yìdiǎn de.

• a little larger	大一点的	dà yìdiǎn de
• a little smaller	小一点的	xiǎo yìdiǎn de
• a little darker	颜色深 一点的	yánsè shēn yìdiǎn de

- a little lighter   颜色浅   yánsè qiǎn
                      一点的   yìdiǎn de
- a little thicker   厚一点的   hòu yìdiǎn de
- a little thinner   薄一点的   bó yìdiǎn de

Please wrap it up.
请 把它包 起来。
Qǐng bǎ tā bāo qǐlái.

Do you have it in a different color?
有 没 有 别的 颜色 的?
Yǒu mei yǒu biéde yánsè de?

Do you have it my size?
有 没 有 我的 尺寸 的?
Yǒu mei yǒu wǒde chǐcùn de?

Can I try it on?
我 可以 试试 吗?
Wǒ kěyǐ shìshi ma?

I found the clothes <u>too large</u>.
我 觉得 这 件 衣服 <u>太大</u>。
Wǒ júede zhè jiàn yīfu <u>tài dà</u>.

- too small   太小   tài xiǎo
- too long   太长   tài cháng
- too short   太短   tài duǎn
- too loose   太肥   tài féi
- too tight   太瘦   tài shòu
- just right   正好   zhèng hǎo

A: What size do you want?
你 要 多 大 号 的?
Nǐ yào duó dà hào de?

B: I want <u>small</u>.
我 要 <u>小 号</u> 的。
Wǒ yào <u>xiǎo hào</u> de.

* medium size   中号   zhōng hào
* large size   大号   dà hào
* extra-large size   特大号   tè dà hào

Please give me a larger/smaller size.
请 给 我 大/小 一 号 的。
Qǐng gěi wǒ dà/xiǎo yí hào de.

How much is this sweater?
这 件 毛衣 多少 钱?
Zhè jiàn máoyī duōshao qián?

A: How much altogether?
一共 多少 钱?
Yígòng duōshǎo qián?

B: It's 53.65.
一共 五十三 块 六 毛 五。
Yígòng wǔshísān kuài liǜ máo wǔ.

Where is the cashier?
付款台 在 哪里?
Fùkuǎntái zài nǎlǐ?

291

Do you accept U.S. dollars?
你们 收 不 收 美元?
Nǐmén shōu bu shōu Měiyuán?

Do you accept credit cards?
你们 收 不 收 信用卡?
Nǐmén shōu bu shōu xìnyòngkǎ?

SIGHTSEEING

I'd like to travel to China.
我 想 去中国 旅行。
Wǒ xiǎng qù Zhōngguó lǚxíng.

Could you recommend some scenic places?
你 能 给我 推荐 风景 好 的
Nǐ néng gěi wǒ tuījiàn fēngjǐng hǎo de
地方 吗?
dìfang ma?

I'd like to go to the Silk Road.
我 想 去 丝绸 之 路。
Wǒ xiǎng qù Sīchóu Zhī Lù.

Do you need a tour guide?
你 需要 导游 吗?
Nǐ xūyào dǎoyóu ma?

Is there a tour guide who can speak English?
有 没 有 会 说 英语 的导游?
Yǒu méi yǒu huì shuō Yīngyǔ de dǎoyóu?

What places of interest are there in this city?
这 个城市 有 什么 <u>名胜</u>
Zhè ge chéngshì yǒu shénme <u>míngshèng</u>
<u>古迹</u>?
<u>gǔjì</u>?

- church　　　　教堂　　　jiàotáng
- gallery　　　　美术馆　　měishùguǎn

293

- museum 博物馆 bówùguǎn
- square 广场 guǎngchǎng
- temple 寺庙 sìyuàn
- park 公园 gōngyuán

When was this building built?
这 座 楼 是 什么 时候 建 的?
Zhè zuò lóu shì shénme shíhou jiàn de?

Whose statue is this?
这 是 谁的 雕像?
Zhè shì shúide diāoxiàng?

What time does the gallery open/close?
美术馆 什么 时候 开门/
Měishùguǎn shénme shíhou kāimén/
关门?
guānmén?

What are the mosque's hours?
清真寺 的 开放 时间 是
Qīngzhēnsì de kāifàng shíjiān shì
什么?
shénme?

Does the museum open on Sunday?
博物馆 星期天 开放 吗?
Bówùguǎn xīngqītiān kāifàng ma?

How much is the admission?
门票 多少 钱?
Ménpiào duōshao qián?

We'd like to go to see the flowers in park.
我们 想 去公园 看 花。
Wǒmen xiǎng qù gōngyuán kàn huā.

I'd like to tour around the city.
我 想 参观 一下市区 风景。
Wǒ xiǎng cānguān yíxià shìqū fēngjǐng.

I need a city map.
我 需要 一 张 市区 地图。
Wǒ xūyào yì zhāng shìqū dìtú.

Where is the entrance/exit?
入口/ 出口 在 哪儿?
Rùkǒu/ chūkǒu zài nǎr?

Can we take pictures here?
这儿 可以 不 可以 照相?
Zhèr kéyǐ bu kéyǐ zhàoxiàng?

Can I have a picture taken with you?
我 能 跟 你照 一 张
Wǒ néng gēn nǐ zhào yì zhāng
照片 吗?
zhàopiàn ma?

Could you take a picture for me?
你 能 帮 我 照 一 张
Nǐ néng bāng wǒ zhào yì zhāng
照片 吗?
zhàopiàn ma?

How beautiful it is here!
这儿 真　漂亮！
Zhèr zhēn piàoliang!

We really love your city.
我们　真　喜欢　你们的　城市。
Wǒmen zhēn xǐhuan nǐmende chéngshì.

How lively is the Confucius Temple!
夫子庙　　真　热闹！
Fūzimiào zhēn rènào!

TRAVEL

Means of transportation

- airplane   飞机   fēijī
- automobile   汽车   qìchē
- bike   自行车   zìxíngchē
- bus   巴士   bāshì
- cab   出租车   chūzūchē
- light rail   轻轨   qīngguǐ
- motor   摩托车   mótuōchē
- ship   船   chuán
- subway   地铁   dìtiě
- train   火车   huǒchē
- van   面包车   miànbāochē

go by plane/ train/ car/ cab/ ship
坐 飞机/火车 /汽车/出租车/ 船   去
zuò fēijī/huǒchē/qìchē/chūzūchē/chuán qù

go by bike/ horse/ motor
骑自行车/ 马/摩托车   去
qí zìxíngchē/mǎ/mótuōchē qù

- arrive   到达   dàodá
- leave   离开   líkāi
- one-way ticket   单程票   dānchéngpiào
- pass   经过   jīngguò
- pick up   接   jiē
- round-trip   双程票   shuāngchéng piào

ticket

- send off 送 sòng
- set out 出发 chūfā
- start 启程 qǐchéng
- stay 逗留 dòuliú
- terminal 终点站 zhōngdiǎnzhàn
- ticket 票 piào
- ticket 售票处 shòupiàochù
  window
- timetable 时刻表 shíkèbiǎo
- transfer 转车 zhuǎnchē

BY AIR

When is the plane to Tokyo taking off?
去 东京　 的 飞机 什么　 时候
Qù Dōngjīng de fēijī shénme shíhou
起飞？
qǐfēi?

Is my flight on time/ delayed?
我的 航班　 正点　 /晚点 吗？
Wǒde hángbān zhèngdiǎn/wǎndiǎn ma?

The flight is canceled.
航班　 取消 了。
Hángbān qǔxiāo le.

Is there any flight to Hangzhou?
有 没 有 去杭州　 的 飞机？
Yǒu méi yǒu qù Hángzhōu de fēijī?

When is the next flight to Beijing?
下 一 班 去 北京　的 飞机 是
Xià yì bān qù Běijīng de fēijī shì
几点？
jǐ diǎn?

How long does it take to fly from Shanghai to Beijing?
坐 飞机 从　上海　　到 北京　要
Zuò fēijī cóng Shànghǎi dào Běijīng yào
多　长　时间？
duō cháng shíjiān?

When will the flight from London arrive?
从　伦敦　来的 航班　几点 到？
Cóng Lúndūn lái de hángbān jǐdiǎn dào?

When will we arrive at Hong Kong?
我们　什么　时候　到 香港？
Wǒmén shénme shíhou dào Xiānggǎng?

BY RAIL

Excuse me, where is the ticket window?
请问，　售票处　在 哪儿？
Qǐngwèn, shòupiàochù zài nǎr?

I want to buy a train ticket to Xi'an.
我 要 买 一张　去 西安 的
Wǒ yào mǎi yì zhāng qù Xī'ān de
火车票。
huǒchēpiào.

Is there a sleeper ticket available?

有 没 有 卧铺票?

Yǒu méi yǒu wòpùpiào?

Excuse me, where is the dining car?

请问， 餐车 在 哪儿?

Qǐngwèn, cānchē zài nǎr?

When is the next train to Suzhou?

下 一 班 去 苏州 的 火车 是

Xià yì bán qù Sūzhōu de huǒchē shì

几点?

jǐdiǎn?

How many trains go to Shanghai from Nanjing per day?

从 南京 去上海 的 火车

Cóng Nánjīng qù Shànghǎi de huǒchē

一 天 有 几班?

yì tiān yǒu jǐ bān?

A: Is this seat taken?

这 个 座位 有 人 坐 吗?

Zhè ge zuòwèi yǒu rén zuò ma?

B: Yes/no.

有/ 没 有。

Yǒu /Méi yǒu.

Can I sit here?

我 可以 坐 在 这儿 吗?

Wǒ kěyǐ zuò zài zhèr ma?

BY BUS & SUBWAY

Excuse me, where is the nearest subway station?

请问， 离 这儿 最 近 的 地铁站

Qǐngwèn, lí zhèr zuì jìn de dìtiězhàn

在 哪儿?

zài nǎr?

Excuse me, where is the No.1 bus stop?

请问， 一 路 公共 汽车站 在

Qǐngwèn, yí lù gōnggòng qìchēzhàn zài

哪儿?

nǎr?

Excuse me, which bus should I take to

请问， 去 动物园 应该 坐

Qǐngwèn, qù dòngwùyuán yīnggāi z

汽车?

qìchē?

Does this bus stop at the Muse

这 路 汽车 去 不 去 历史博

Zhè lù qìchē qù bu qù Lìshǐ

Where can I take the bus
University?

我 在 哪儿 可以 坐

Wǒ zài nǎr kěyǐ zu

汽车?

qìchē?

Please let me know when it arrives at the Bund.

到 外滩 时，请 告诉 我。

Dào Wàitān shí, qǐng gàosù wǒ.

I want to get off at the People's Park.

要 在 人民 公园 下 车。

o zài Rénmín Gōngyuán xià chē.

d a cab?

叫 到 出租车？

dào chūzūchē?

the zoo?

几路

uō jǐ lù

车 吗

hē ma?

m of History?

博物馆？

Bówùguǎn?

o Nanjing

南京 大学 的

o qù Nanjing Dàxué de

Keep straight ahead.
一直 向　前 开！
Yìzhí xiàng qián kāi!

Stop!
停！
Tíng!

How much should I pay you?
我　该 付你 多少　钱？
Wǒ gāi fù nǐ duōshao qián?

Keep the change.
不用　找　钱 了。
Búyòng zhǎo qián le.

IMMIGRATION

A: Do you have anything to declare?
你 有 东西 要 申报 吗?
Nǐ yǒu dōngxi yào shēnbào ma?

B: Yes/no.
有/ 没 有。
Yǒu/Méi yǒu.

Please show me your passport.
请 给 我 看看 你 的 护照。
Qǐng gěi wǒ kànkan nǐde hùzhào.

How long will you stay here?
你 要 在 这里 逗留 多 久?
Nǐ yào zài zhèlǐ dòuliú duōjiǔ?

Must I pay duties on this?
这 件 物品 我 必须 交 税 吗?
Zhè jiàn wùpǐn wǒ bìxū jiāo shuì ma?

Could you please tell me how to fill out this form?
请 告诉 我 怎么 填 这 张 表。
Qǐng gàosù wǒ zěnme tián zhè zhāng biǎo.

Can I fill out the form in English?
可以 用 英文 填 这 张 表 吗?
Kěyǐ yòng Yīngwén tián zhè zhāng biǎo ma?

Where can I get the Entry & Exit Permit Form?
我 在 哪儿 可以 拿 到 出入境 表?
Wǒ zài nǎr kěyǐ ná dào chūrùjìng biǎo?

USEFUL WORDS & EXPRESSIONS

• address	地址/住址	dìzhǐ/zhùzhǐ
• age	年龄	niánlíng
• birthday	出生日期	chūshēng rìqī
• citizen	公民	gōngmín
• date	日期	rìqī
• destination	前往地/ 目的地	qiánwǎng dì/ mùdìdì
• documents	证件	zhèngjiàn
• document number	证件号码	zhèngjiàn hàomǎ
• document type	证件种类	zhèngjiàn zhǒnglèi
• family name	姓	xìng
• first name	名	míng
• fill in	填写	tiánxiě
• flight number	航班号	hángbān hào
• gender	性别	xìngbié
• marital status	婚姻状况	hūnyīn zhuàngkuàng
o married	已婚	yǐhūn
o single	单身	dānshēn
o unmarried	未婚	wèihūn
• nationality	国籍	guójí
• occupation	职业	zhíyè
• passport number	护照号码	hùzhào hàomǎ
• permanent resident	永久居民	yǒngjiǔ jūmín

305

- place of birth | 出生地 | chūshēngdì
- purpose | 事由 | shìyóu
  - o business | 商务 | shāngwù
  - o employment | 就业 | jiùyè
  - o immigration | 定居 | dìngjū
  - o others | 其他 | qítā
  - o sightsee | 观光/旅 | guānguāng/ lǚyóu
  - o study | 学习 | xuéxí
  - o visit family | 探亲 | tànqīn
  - o visit | 访问 | fǎngwèn
  - o work | 工作 | gōngzuò
- ship name | 船名 | chuán míng
- signature | 签名 | qiānmíng
- State Administration for Entry/Exit | 出入境 管理局 | Chūrùjìng Guǎnlǐjú
- train/bus number | 车次 | chēcì
- visa | 签证 | qiānzhèng
  - o business visa | 商务签证 | shāngwù qiānzhèng
  - o student visa | 学习签证 | xuéxí qiānzhèng
  - o tourist visa | 旅游签证 | lǚyóu qiānzhèng
  - o work visa | 工作签证 | gōngzuò qiānzhèng